Computer-Based National Information Systems

With an
Introduction by
Stephen J. Andriole

A Source Book

PBI
a petrocelli
book
new york / princeton

Printed in the United States of America.
1 2 3 4 5 6 7 8 9 10

This book was originally published, in a different form, by the Office of Technology Assessment for the Congress of the United States.

Library of Congress Cataloging in Publication Data
Main entry under title:

Computer-based national information systems.

"A Petrocelli book."
1. Computer networks. 2. Information services and state—United States. I. Andriole, Stephen J.
TK5105.5.C6363 1984 025'.04'0973 84-5908
ISBN 0-89433-255-4

Editor's Introduction

It is to the credit of the Congress' Office of Technology Assessment (OTA) that it undertook this study on the nature and function of the computer-based national information systems that affect so many of our lives. The technological and public policy issues discussed in this study are timely and—perhaps surprisingly—terribly under-analyzed. It seems that during the past two decades or so we have been overtaken by computer and related technologies to the point that many of us know something about the computer-based national information systems now in use, but we know very little about how dramatically these systems have changed, challenged, and in some cases threatened our lives. For example; How many of us really understand how large data bases comprised of information about our voting or spending habits are distributed throughout the country? How many of us have considered just how dependent we all are upon the accuracy and efficiency of air traffic control systems? What about security and privacy? Can we be sure that only authorized users are operating the systems or, like so many seem to fear, are the databases being used to curtail our freedoms? What about governmental regulatory policy? Can our regulatory systems handle the challenges of the information society? Should whole sections of the constitution be reinterpreted with reference to the development and use of computer-based information systems?

Among other concerns, this study suggests that our freedoms of speech and press, our constitutional protection against unreasonable search and seizure, and our guarantees against self-incrimination and access to due process of law may all be challenged by the continued proliferation of larger and more powerful national information systems. In a few short years it will be possible to locate and access all kinds of data on all kinds of behaviors. While such progress may make it painless to place a genuinely confirmed airline reservation, it may also centralize access to information about our personal habits.

Computer-Based National Information Systems is the first study of its kind. It is the result of the efforts of innumerable experts in many diverse fields. In order to complete the project, a National Information Systems Advisory Panel along with a Special Advisory Panel in Information Technology were established. The insights provided by members of these panels were gathered, evaluated, and synthesized by OTA's National Information Systems Assessment and Publishing staffs, and before its release it was reviewed by OTA's Technology Assessment Board. By design, the study raises as many questions as it answers. Indeed, had its results been conclusive it would have fallen far short of its goal. Instead, it successfully illuminates the technology that underlies the development of computer-based national information systems and calls attention to the public policy issues triggered by their use.

Another major contribution of the study lies in its *formalization* of a discussion that has proceeded without real direction for far too long. Up until the publication of this study one would have to search far and wide for the materials and ideas presented in *Computer-Based National Information Systems.* The study thus serves simultaneously as a reference guide and as a forum for future discussion and debate.

In keeping with these goals the study is well-organized and well-written. It does not assume that the reader is knowledgeable in computer or information science; nor does it require enthusiasm for the nuances and details of public policy analysis. It is highly focused and deals only with those areas necessary to accomplish its mission. Three cases in point are Chapters 1, 2, and 3. Chapter 1 presents a summary of the entire study. Chapter 2 provides you with a detailed look at its background and purpose, while Chapter

3 introduces the layman to the nature of computers and computer-based national information systems. It is thus impossible to become lost within or confused by the study.

This study also takes on the tough issues. Entire chapters are devoted to privacy, security, constitutional rights, and regulatory policy. It far from shrinks from the reality of our dependence upon computer-based national information systems, noting with alarm the problems connected with our air traffic control and national defense early warning systems.

The last two chapters of the study are especially valuable in and of themselves, and are stepping stones to more detailed analysis. Chapter 13 deals with trends in computer technology and with the relationships between computer technology and the design, development, and use of computer-based information systems. Chapter 13 suggests that first generation national information systems will be replaced by future generations with far more power and "friendliness" than their predecessors. It also deals with the implications of those trends. Chapter 14 looks at the very structure of the electronic data processing industry, generally, and with specific reference to the development of national information systems. Like Chapter 13, this final chapter is so well done that regardless of your interest in computer-based national information systems you will find it valuable.

Our decision to publish a commercial version of this excellent OTA study was very straightforward. *Computer-Based National Information Systems* is unique and important. It is also well-organized and well-written. But like many excellent government-sponsored reports, without commercial distribution it would probably only reach a small part of its potential audience. Hopefully this commercial version will reach a much wider audience and stimulate an even larger analysis and debate.

Stephen J. Andriole

Foreword

This report presents the results of an overview study on the use of computer technology in national information systems and related public policy issues. The purposes of this study are:

- *To provide a general introduction to computer-based national information systems.*—Will help acquaint the nonexpert reader with the nature of computer-based national information systems and the role they play in American society.
- *To provide a framework for understanding computer and information policy issues.*—Develops a structure of information policy and presents brief essays on several of the more important issue areas, with an emphasis on how future applications of computer-based information systems may intensify or alter the character of the policy debate and the need for new or revised laws and policies.
- *To provide a state-of-the-art survey of computer and related technologies and industries.*—Highlights recent developments in computer and information technologies and describes the current status and likely evolution of the computer and information industries.
- *To provide a foundation for other related studies.* While some observations can be made about national information systems in general, a full assessment of impacts and issues is best conducted in the context of specific systems. The report builds a foundation for three related OTA studies in the areas of computerized criminal history records, electronic mail, and electronic funds transfer. These three separate studies will be published later this year.

As a set, the four studies comprise the OTA assessment of Societal Impacts of National Information Systems that was requested by the Senate Committee on the Judiciary, House Committee on the Judiciary, and House Post Office and Civil Service Committee. Supporting requests were received from the House Government Operations Subcommittee on Government Information and Individual Rights and the House Science and Technology Subcommittee on Science, Research, and Technology.

OTA appreciates the participation of the many advisory panelists and others who helped bring this study to completion.

JOHN H. GIBBONS
Director

Acknowledgments

The following individuals contributed as contractors or reviewers during the course of the study:

Charles C. Joyce and Jeffrey Held, Richard L. Deal & Associates, Inc.
Kenneth C. Laudon, Croton Research Group, Inc.
Donald A. Marchand, University of South Carolina at Columbia
Jeffrey A. Meldman, Massachusetts Institute of Technology
Fred Bernard Wood, Computer Social Impact Research Institute, Inc.
John L. King and Kenneth L. Kraemer, Irvine Research Corp.
Fred M. Greguras, Kutak, Rock & Huie
Alan Lipis, Electronic Banking, Inc.

Contents

Overview

Computers have become a major technological tool of American society during the last quarter of a century. New developments in computer and communication technology promise within this decade an even more radical revolution in the way that information is collected, stored, used, and disseminated.

Large-scale integrated circuit technology, for example, allows hundreds of thousands of electronic components to be fabricated on a thin wafer smaller than a paper clip, thereby providing computing capability hundreds of times less expensive, less energy-consuming, and more reliable than was available only two or three decades ago. One result is the rapid growth in small, inexpensive computers that are the equivalent of machines selling for as much as a million dollars in the 1950's. Data communication networks using satellite and microwave technologies make it possible to provide access economically to large data bases from anywhere in the country or the world. Thus, networks of remotely sited computers can provide services such as credit card and check authorization or airline scheduling to users nationwide.

As these and other computer-based information systems—such as those used in air traffic control, military command and control, and electronic funds transfer—become more important to American society, they create corresponding public policy issues. Among the most important issues are the following:

- *Innovation, productivity, and employment.*—Continued innovation in information technology is a prime requisite for a healthy information industry and also offers the tools for improving the productivity of many other sectors of the economy. Likely policy issues include: support for research and development on civilian applications of computer technology, vitality of academic computer science, support for computer impact research (e.g., the impact on employment), and maintaining U.S. international competitiveness in computers and information systems.
- *Privacy.*—New applications of computer and communication technology—e.g., an automated securities exchange, in-home information services, electronic publishing, and the automated office—may generate issues over secondary use of personal information, surveillance, and the possible need for new approaches to privacy policy.
- *Security.*—The technology for securing computer systems from theft, sabotage, natural hazards, privacy abuses, and the like is improving steadily. However, the increasingly complicated systems now being designed and built make secure operations more difficult and suggest likely issues concerning the adequate protection of Federal information systems and vital non-Federal systems, and the development of the necessary data security and cryptographic capability.
- *Government management of data processing.*—It appears that, in general, the Federal Government is rapidly falling behind the private sector in its use and management of up-to-date computer and information technology. The 96th Congress enacted Public Law 96-511 (Paperwork Reduction Act of 1980) to help address this problem. And other issues may arise with respect to the effects of large-scale information systems on Federal decisionmaking (the "automated bureaucracy") and the process by which social values are reflected in information system design.

- *Society's dependence on information systems.*—As society moves toward electronic mail and other large extensively used information systems, likely new issues will concern the ways in which public policy can help balance the risks society may encounter versus the benefits, retain the option to end dependence on a particular system (avoid becoming "locked in"), and provide alternatives for those who prefer not to use electronic services. Research on the risks of system failure is needed, as is careful attention to how technology can be used to reduce these risks (for example, through distributed data bases and back-up computers).
- *Constitutional rights.*—Little legal precedent exists, in many cases, for applying constitutional law to issues raised by computer-based information systems. Areas of constitutional rights that may be affected by information systems include: freedom of speech and press (first amendment), protection against unreasonable search and seizure (fourth), protection against self-incrimination and guarantee of due process of law (fifth), right to a trial by impartial jury (sixth), and State guarantees of due process and equal protection of the laws (14th).
- *Regulatory boundaries.*—Evolving computer-based systems are crossing over and blurring traditional regulatory boundaries. Regulatory policy issues are likely to recur with respect to computer- v. communication-based services, electronic interstate branch banking, and electronic mail. As these systems expand geographically and move away from traditional definitions of industry structure, policy issues concerning interstate conflict of laws, Federal-State relationships, and antitrust may also arise.
- *Other issues.*—Four other issue areas were identified as important although not analyzed in great detail: computer crime, transborder data flow, information gap (for those who would be denied access due to technological illiteracy or other reasons), and computer software protection.

Chapter 1
Summary

Contents

TABLE

LIST OF FIGURES

Chapter 1
Summary

Introduction

Computers and Information Systems

Computers have become a major technological tool of American society during the past quarter of a century. New developments in computer and communication technology promise within this decade an even more radical revolution in the way that information is collected, stored, used, and disseminated.

Large-scale integrated circuit technology allows hundreds of thousands of electronic components to be fabricated on a thin silicon wafer smaller than a paper clip (see fig. 1) thus providing computing capability hundreds of times less expensive, less energy-consuming, and more reliable than was available only two or three decades ago, as shown in figure 2. Because these microelectronic devices are changing the economics of computer access and use, they are dramatically

Figure 1.—The One-Chip Computer: Offspring of the Transistor

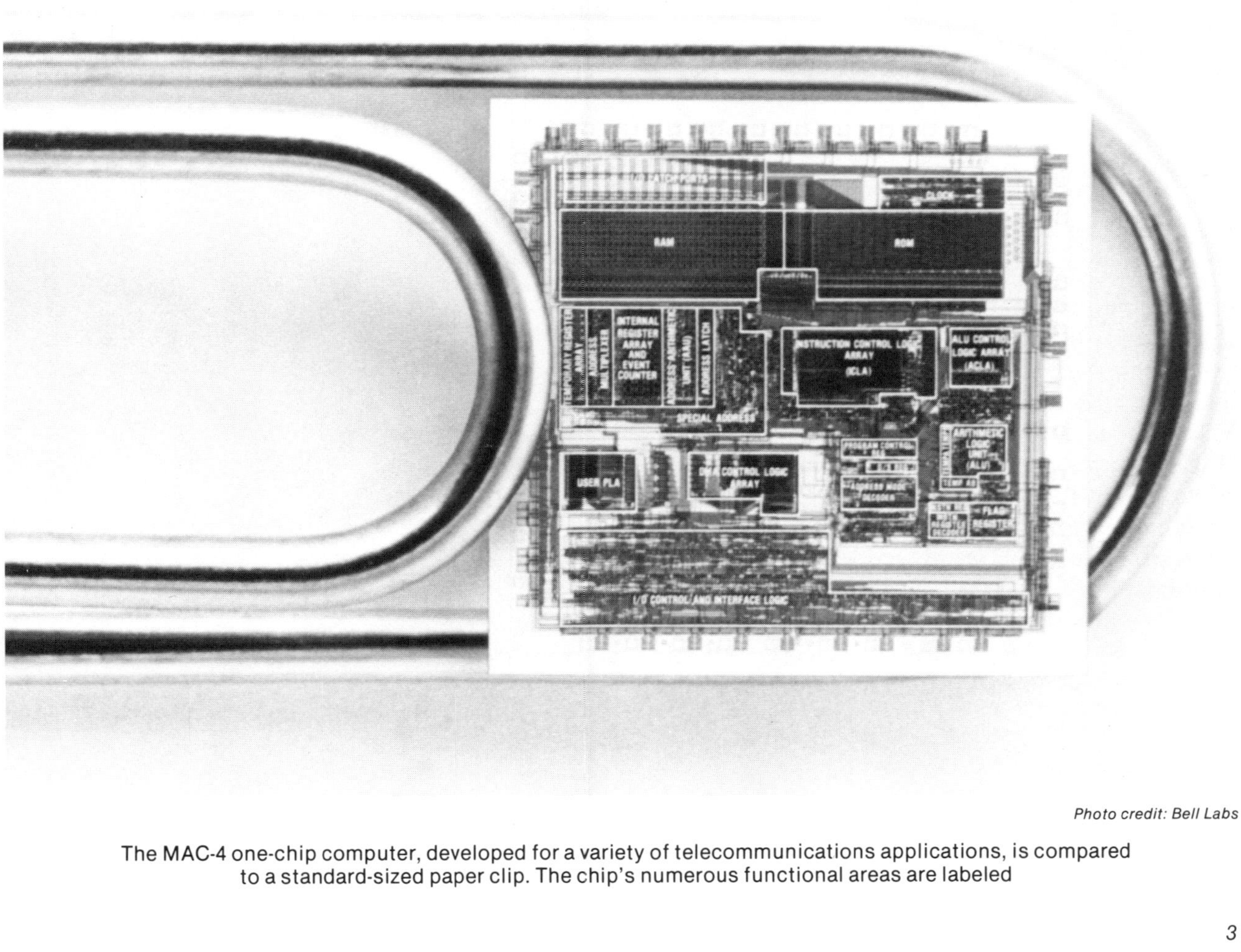

Photo credit: Bell Labs

The MAC-4 one-chip computer, developed for a variety of telecommunications applications, is compared to a standard-sized paper clip. The chip's numerous functional areas are labeled

Figure 2.—Drop in Average Computer System Cost per 100,000 Calculations From 1952-80

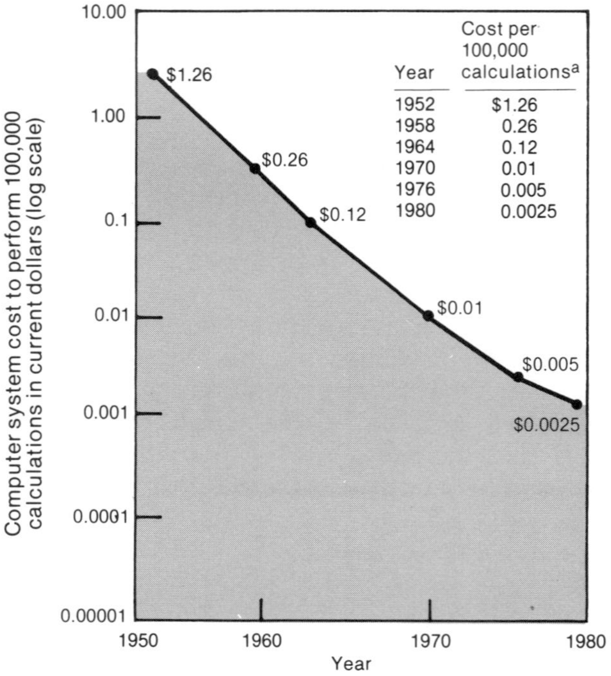

[a]Cost per 100,000 calculations is based on data for the following IBM computer systems (with year in parentheses): 701 (1952), 7090 (1958), 360/50 (1964), 370/166 (1970), 3033 (1976), 4300 (1980).

SOURCE: Office of Technology Assessment and President's Reorganization Project, *Federal Data Processing Reorganization Study: Basic Report of the Science and Technology Team*, Washington, D.C., June 1978, pp. 29-30.

affecting the ways in which computers are used, and who is using them.

This change has been accompanied by equally rapid improvement in communication technology.* New telecommunication technologies such as direct satellite broadcasting, local area distribution cables, and long-distance data communication networks allow computers to be used in ways that were unimagined a decade ago. Although initially distinctly different, computer and communication technologies are increasingly interdependent, and are being combined to form new products and services and to change the nature of information systems in several ways:

- Computers are becoming smaller and less expensive, thereby increasing their range of applications. Today, computer logic is even being built into common devices such as ovens and automobile carburetors, and complete small computer systems are being sold through consumer retail outlets at a price equivalent to a first-rate high-fidelity stereo set. At the center of this transformation is the integrated circuit chip, a tiny device capable of containing an entire computer system. The increasing capability of these circuit chips is shown in figure 3. As a result, the large computer that occupied one or several rooms in the late 1960's will soon fit in a desk drawer, and a medium-size computer will fit in a briefcase or even a coat pocket.
- Computers can be connected inexpensively to communication lines making it possible to provide access economically to large computer data bases from any-

Figure 3.—Increase in Capability of Semiconductor Chips From 1956-80

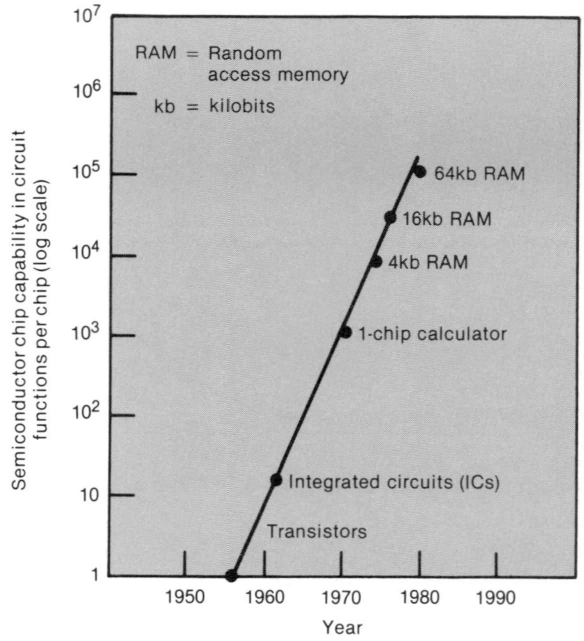

SOURCE: Institute of Electrical and Electronic Engineers, *IEEE Spectrum*, vol. 17, June 1980, p. 48; and "VLSI/LSI" *IEEE Spectrum*, vol. 18, January 1981, pp. 57-61.

*The development of communication technology is examined in detail in the OTA report, *Telecommunication Technology and Public Policy*, in press.

where in the country or the world. Networks of remotely sited computers provide services such as credit card and check authorization or airline scheduling to users nationwide.

- Techniques for the organization and display of information are improving as are methods of instructing the computer to perform its tasks, thus making it easier for nonexperts to obtain usable information.
- Information storage technology which is less costly and more compact makes it feasible to store large amounts of information for long periods of time in electronic form. In many cases it costs less for electronic storage than to maintain paper records, and access to specific items is faster and more accurate.

National Information Systems

The focus of this study is on national information systems that are made possible by advances in computer and communication technology.

The term "national information systems" as used here means systems that: are substantially national in geographic scope (i.e., multistate); are organized by Government or private organizations or groups to collect, store, manipulate, and disseminate information about persons and/or institutions; and are in some significant manner based on computers and related information and com munication technology.

Furthermore, the focus is primarily on large, interconnected national systems where a substantial national interest is involved (e.g., in the financial, postal, military, and air traffic safety areas). Examples of such systems include:

- the computer-based National Crime Information Center operated by the Federal Bureau of Investigation;
- the FEDWIRE electronic funds transfer network operated by the Federal Reserve System;
- the nationwide electronic mail services operated by several private firms and soon to involve the U.S. Postal Service;
- the nationwide computer-based credit card and check authorization services (e.g., VISA, American Express, MasterCard, Telecheck, Telecredit);
- the computerized air traffic control system operated by the Federal Aviation Administration;
- the computerized military command and control systems operated by the Department of Defense;
- the nationwide computer-based airline reservation systems operated by major air carriers (e.g., United, TWA, American); and
- the computerized automatic quotation system for obtaining over-the-counter stock prices operated by the National Association of Securities Dealers.

A secondary focus of the study is on the use of personal computers* when interconnected as part of a larger network. For example, MicroNet and The Source are new services designed to link owners of personal computers with each other and with larger computers, data banks, and information processing services, over a nationwide network. Also, in the future, stand-alone computer games when combined, for instance, with a television set and a telephone will be able to serve as a terminal with similar access to a nationwide network.

A typical national information system is illustrated in figures 4 and 5. In the example, there are seven cities (nodes) in the network: New York, Washington, D.C., Chicago, Dallas, Atlanta, Los Angeles, and San Francisco. Information (for instance, on inventory, sales, credit transactions, and the like) is stored by the headquarters office of a national retail sales company in a central (host) computer in Dallas, as shown in figure 4. The regional offices also store information in

*Small but fully capable computers currently selling for several hundred to a few thousand dollars and designed for use by individuals in the home, business, or school.

Figure 4.—Computer Technology in a National Information System (illustrative)

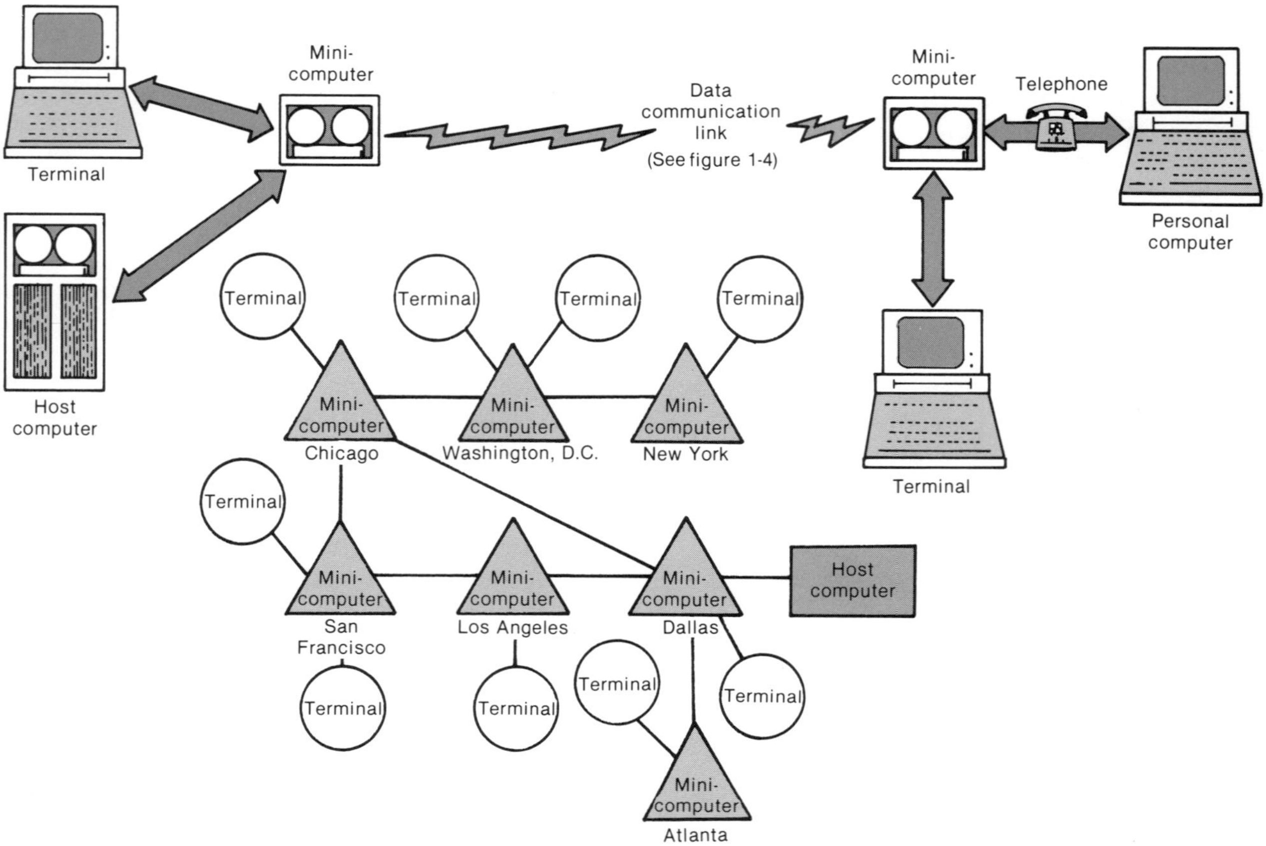

SOURCE: Office of Technology Assessment based on *IEEE Spectrum*, vol. 17, October 1980, p. 24; and ARINC Corp., *Overview of Domestic Telecommunications Common Carrier Industry*, September 1979.

their own minicomputers.* All terminals on the network can access the headquarters data base (in the host computer) and the regional data bases distributed around the country. The information is disseminated from one city to another via the satellite and microwave communication links illustrated in figure 5.

This is an example of current technology used by a growing number of private firms and some Government agencies in what is known as a "distributed data processing network." Distributed means that the data bases (and computer capability) can be in several locations (e.g., branches of a retail store as above, or regional offices of a Government agency) rather than in one central computer. Furthermore, owners of a personal computer could plug into such a network, with the appropriate code words and authorization, via a telephone line (see fig. 4) in their own home or office and actually transact business by computer.

*Small computer systems currently selling for under $50,000.

Purpose and Limitations of the Study

This overview study is intended to be a broad introductory examination of computer-based national information systems and related technology and public policy issues that Congress is likely to face over the next few years. It will also serve as a foundation for the other OTA information systems studies and for future in-depth examination

Figure 5.—Communication Technology in a National Information System (illustrative)

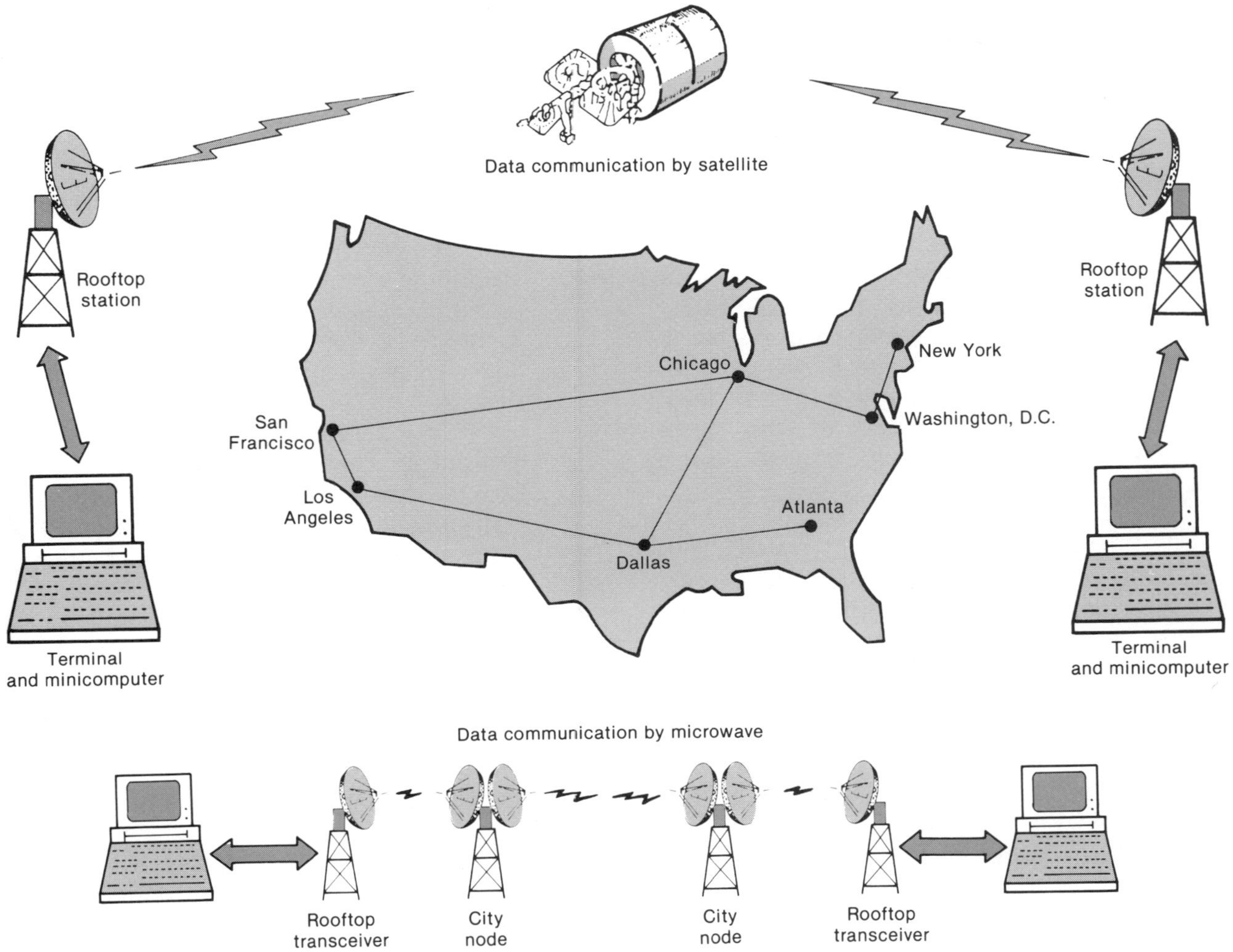

SOURCE: Office of Technology Assessment based on *IEEE Spectrum*, vol. 17, October 1980, p. 24; and ARINC Corp., *Overview of Domestic Telecommunications Common Carrier Industry*, September 1979.

of particular systems and issues. It also examines the increasingly critical role that national information systems play in society.

It would not be possible for any one study to capture succinctly a single set of policy issues that would apply to all national information systems in American society. The specific system applications are too diverse, the potentials and problems too complex, and the parties-at-interest and relevant institutional and legal frameworks too disparate. Only a few of the many issues examined in this study will be important for any particular system.

Consequently, OTA is also conducting case studies of three specific national information systems:

1. an assessment of the National Crime Information Center Computerized Criminal History System;
2. a preliminary assessment of the role of the U.S. Postal Service in electronic message systems; and
3. a preliminary assessment of electronic funds transfer systems.

These case studies will provide a more detailed look at the impacts and issues associated with a specific national information system.

Computers, Information Systems, and Society

Nature of Computer-Based Information Systems

Traditionally, computers have been viewed as super calculators that automate processes that were previously performed by people sitting at mechanical adding machines. However, computers carry out a wide variety of tasks associated with processing information. It is important to understand the entire range of these capabilities in order to appreciate the nature and magnitude of the potential social impacts of this technology when used in information systems.

Computer capabilities fall into seven main categories:

1. *Data collection.* When attached to various sensing devices, computers can detect and measure such external physical phenomena as temperature, time, pressure, flow rate, or any number of other variables. Also, computers can keep a record of transactions. For example, a computerized cash register can collect and store information about a sale that includes bookkeeping entries, taxes, commissions and inventory, and can even reorder stock. Some computer-based door locks require individuals to carry magnetic identity cards. Such locks not only can control access but also can create a record of whose card was granted access, when, and for how long.

   Technological advances are beginning to provide computers with the capability to directly process visual and audio input, thus greatly increasing their applicability to data collection. Computers already have a limited ability to recognize human speech, to read directly a variety of typewritten forms and handprinted texts, and to detect patterns in video images. These functions will be improving rapidly over the next decade and will soon appear in commercial equipment.
2. *Information storage.* Computers can store large amounts of information for long periods of time in an electronically readable form that is easily and quickly recoverable. Depending on the particular application, the methods of storage vary widely, from signals in electronic circuitry, to magnetic pulses on tape, to holes in cards. New advances in memory technology eventually will allow trillions of characters of information to be stored conveniently and cheaply wherever there is even a small computer. The cost of storing information electronically will soon be substantially lower than the cost of storing the same amount of information on paper.
3. *Information organization.* Computers can be used to rearrange information so that it is more suitable for particular applications. For example, if the data in a telephone directory were stored in a computer's memory, it could be inverted to allow one to look up a telephone number that corresponds to a particular address. More generally, computers can simplify and restructure vast amounts of raw data to assist people in drawing significant meanings or conclusions.
4. *Calculations.* Computers perform arithmetic calculations millions of times faster than can human beings. They are used to make numerous simple calculations, such as those required in processing the payroll for a sizable organization; to make sophisticated statistical calculations on large amounts of data, such as those for social science research; or to perform highly complex scientific calculations, such as those needed for weather research or for modeling fusion energy systems.
5. *Communication.* Through connections over a communication system, computers can transmit data around the Nation and the world either to human users or to other computers, which per-

mits the sharing of work and data among groups of linked computers (known as computer networking). Private firms are beginning to offer special communication services to support computer networking. In addition, computers make possible the more effective use and management of the communication systems themselves.

6. *Information presentation.* Computers can put out information in a variety of forms. Through graphical display, and more recently through voice response, they can make data readily understandable and useful to nonexperts. It is possible to display data and computer schematics on screens in a multicolored, three-dimensional format for design and analytical purposes. Also, data such as numbers and statistics can be organized by the computer in an easy-to-understand tabular presentation. Much of the programing effort in developing modern management information is directed toward designing ways in which the information generated by the computer can be presented most clearly to the manager who needs it.
7. *Control.* Computers can be used to control a machine tool or a production line without human intervention. Many consumer devices—including microwave ovens, automated home thermostats, automobile engines, television sets, and telephones—incorporate computer controls using new microprocessor technology. Such uses are increasing rapidly.

Future Trends in Computer-Based Information Systems

The use of computers during the 1980's will likely follow the key trends discussed below and covered in depth in chapters 13 and 14.

- *Growth in the use of personal computers.* The small computer will become common both in the home and in business. Despite their small size, these systems will be highly capable—the equivalent of machines that sold for as much as a million dollars in the 1950's. They may appear in the guise of video games, television sets, or telephones that will also have a computer capability available for other purposes. This trend will stimulate more widespread computer literacy in society, and in turn be reinforced by the consequent increase in the ability of people to program and use computers. The first generation to grow up with computers is now reaching maturity. These "computer literate" young adults accept computers as a natural part of their world. Computer design and use will be taught more both in school and as part of adult education, and will enhance an already thriving market for specialized application programs designed for small computers.

Photo credit: Texas Instruments, Inc.

INSIGHT Series 10 Personal Information Terminal. Standing only 12 inches high with a 5½-inch swivel display screen

- *Expansion in the number and size of computer networks.* By the end of the decade, most computers, even small ones, will be connected to a communication network at least part of the time.

  The communication system may be dedicated to a single application in which all the machines on the network perform portions of a larger task. Public data networks, on the other hand, provide any home or business computer with access to a wide range of data bases or special programs that may be wanted for occasional use. Such multiuser national networks that can be interconnected now exist, and the number of users is expected to grow at a rapid rate.

- *The trend toward information services.* The computer industry has traditionally been concerned with selling hardware (desktop, mini, and mainframe computers and related auxiliary equipment). However, current trends in both pricing and the structure of the market are driving the emphasis toward providing computer-based information services, such as bibliographic and data base searches, electronic publishing, electronic banking, and the like. A number of these services will still require that the user possess a computer. However, many will be offered over data communication lines to homes and offices, and will be accessible through a modified ("intelligent") telephone or television set. Examples include two-way cable television, videotext, and the AT&T Electronic Information Services experiment that provides an electronic telephone directory over a telephone line to a home terminal. Eventually, information services of all kinds will dominate the data processing market in terms of dollar volume.
- *The competition among giant corporations for the data communication services market.* IBM, AT&T, Exxon, and GTE, among others, are preparing to offer a variety of data communication services. Large corporations such as these have access to the capital required to install the technological base for the planned services, such as communication satellite systems and fiber optic transmission lines. A series of recent rulings by the FCC, some still under challenge, are intended to clear the way for open competition among these and other corporations to provide information services of all kinds over communication lines. Resolution of the pending challenges by the courts or by Congress will have significant implications over the long term for the data communication industry.*
- *Higher level integration of data services.* Many individual networks for servicing specific corporate and governmental needs will continue to be built. Some of these networks will become integrated. For example, most airlines, car rental agencies, and large hotel chains have their own reservation systems. It is now technically feasible to build an integrated system that would provide travel agents access to all of these reservation systems through one desktop terminal.

  Similar integrated information systems are also feasible in insurance, banking, travel, entertainment, law enforcement, commodities exchanges, medical services, and many other sectors that now use several separate information systems. However, implementation of these systems will depend on perceived need, economic viability, and other related factors.
- *The software bottleneck.* According to many computer and industry experts, the increasing capability of computer hardware is not being fully utilized due to problems encountered in creating suitable software programs for these new machines. The major problems are the relatively slow increase in the productivity of programers—their cost efficiency—compared with that of the hardware, and the difficulties encountered in managing large programing projects.

  These problems have created bottlenecks in the development of new applications. Computer programing has been relatively resistant to productivity improvement, at least when compared with corresponding improvements in hardware performance. Programing is by nature labor intensive. Its cost is rising due to the increased programing requirements of new hardware coupled with a shortage of programing personnel with the required training and experience. New mechanisms

*For a detailed discussion, see the OTA report *Telecommunication Technology and Public Policy,* in press.

Photo credit: Office of Technology Assessment staff

Integrated information systems will allow for on-line access to all stock exchanges

such as structured programing will be helpful in engineering computer programs and managing their design and implementation.

At the other end of the scale, microtechnology is making possible enormous increases in computational power through the creation of new hardware structures from clusters of small computer chips. Technologists know how to physically construct such combinations, but not how to use them as effectively as their potential would suggest.

Eliminating software bottlenecks may be the key to maintaining the lead in computer technology in the coming decade. In Japan, for example, the software problem has now been given a very high priority for research and development (R&D). In the United States, although a few defense agencies are investing in research to solve some of the problems, Federal R&D budgets for computer science and technology have not accorded software a similar priority. Private industry is the source of most activity in this area. Reportedly, one-third of the research effort at Bell Labs is devoted to the software problem.

The Computer-Based Information Society

An information industry analyst recently observed that "every society is an information society."* That is, all human organizations, no matter how simple, depend for their functioning on an intangible resource called "information." In any society, information serves several purposes. It can be, for example, a commodity of commerce, an indicator of wealth or power, a basis for making decisions, or a source of entertainment.

Several key trends are transforming the United States into a computer-based information society:

- *The tasks being undertaken by the large organizations that serve American society are growing in complexity.* The air traffic control system handles nearly 20 million flights yearly. Every year the financial system clears over 30 billion checks, the U.S. Postal Service delivers over 100 billion pieces of mail, and the Internal Revenue Service (IRS) receives more than 140 million tax returns. The use of computer-based systems is one way to cope with this vast and complex information flow.
- *The service sector of the economy is growing at a relatively faster rate than the industrial and agricultural sectors.* Many services such as medicine, law, education, and Government involve the transfer of large amounts of information. Resistance to productivity improvements in this sector, which represents a large part of the economy, has impeded overall productivity growth. Greater application of information technology has been proposed as a chief remedy. For this reason, it is highly likely that in this decade the service sector will increasingly depend on the use of computer-based information systems.
- *The information sector itself has grown to account for over half of the U.S. work force.* An examination of the trends in the work force reveals the extent to which the economy has shifted. The results shown graphically in figure 6 illustrate the transitions from an economy dominated by agriculture, to one dominated by manufacturing, to a service and information economy.

  The information sector includes those who generate and sell information as well as those who produce information technology. Included are typewriter and word processor manufacturers, newspaper publishers, and producers of films and broadway and television shows, all of whom are rapidly incorporating computer-based information systems into their operations. The information sector also covers information services and products used by any organization for its own internal purposes. Examples are internal accounting and production management, and inventory control systems, many of which are already computerized.
- *Greater international economic competition coupled with the decreasing availability of basic resources are requiring industry and Government to both improve and speed up their decisionmaking capabilities.* Computer-based information systems are growing in importance for this purpose. Decisions about design, marketing, financing, and resource allocation all require a more sophisticated approach to the collection and use of information.

*Anthony G. Oettinger, "Information Resources: Knowledge and Power in the 21st Century," *Science Magazine*, vol. 209, July 1980, p. 191.

Figure 6.—Four Sector Aggregation of the U.S. Work Force by Percent, 1860-1980

(Using median estimates of information workers)

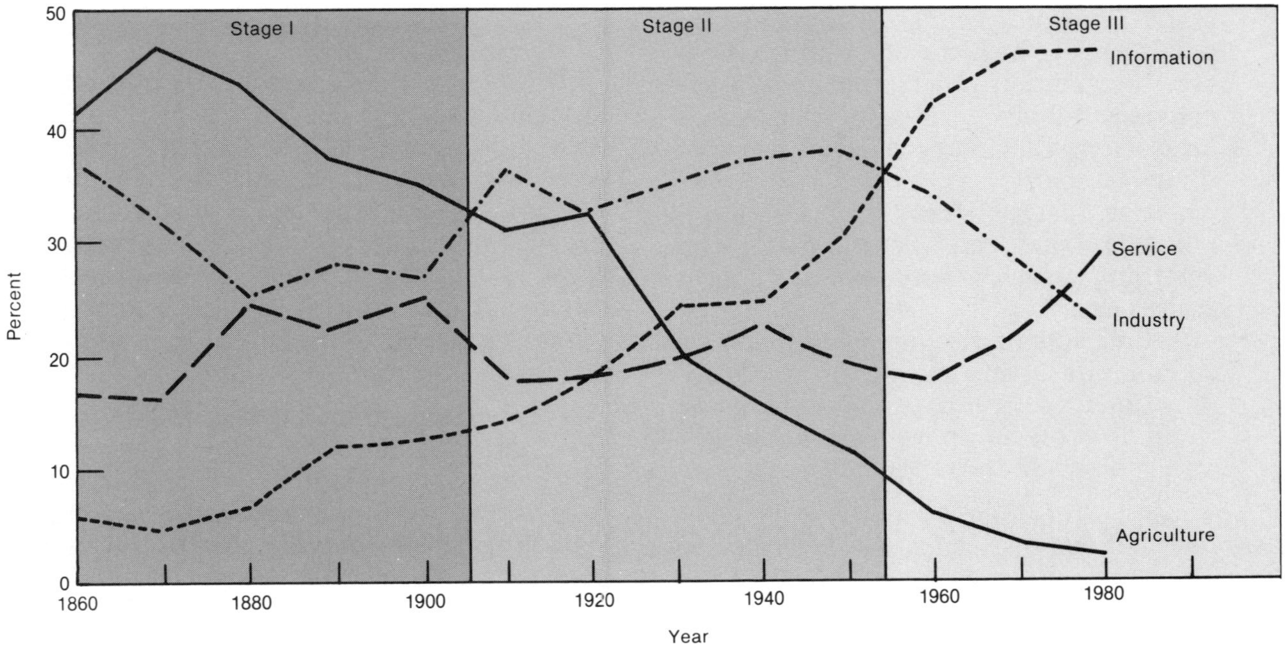

SOURCE: Marc V. Porat, *The Information Economy,* Stanford University Institute for Communication Research, report no. 27, vol. 1, p. 189, August 1976. See ch. 4 for further discussion.

The Structure of Information Policy Issues

Information Policy, Law, and Regulation

As these computer-based systems become more important to American society, particularly for Government administration, they create corresponding public policy issues. Current policies governing information systems are a composite of many specific regulations and laws, which are based on three main factors:

1. the areas affected or the regulatory concerns (privacy, freedom of information, etc.);
2. the affected sector of society (banking, education, Government, etc.); and
3. the lawmakers and/or rulemakers (Congress, the Federal Communications Commission (FCC), State legislatures, the Courts, etc.)

In the course of this study, OTA identified 14 major areas of law and regulation* that affect information systems or are affected by them. There are undoubtedly many others.

The analysis made by OTA has led to these findings:

- There are numerous laws and regulations, some overlapping and some potentially or actually conflicting, that directly and indirectly affect the operators and users of information systems, the consumers of information

*These areas are privacy, freedom of information, first amendment, 14th amendment, due process, communication regulation (Computer II decision of the FCC), computer crime, proprietary rights (patent, trademark, copyright), evidence, liability, antitrust, taxation, Government provision of information, and Government procurement of information systems.

services, and the subjects of personal information data banks.

- There appears to be neither a strong trend nor sentiment at present among policymakers in favor of a uniform Federal information policy that would encompass all the problems that could arise from the many possible uses of data systems.*
- There is a lack of focus on information policy as such, and consequently the emerging issues are not being directly addressed.**
- Continuation of the present situation could inhibit many socially desirable applications of information systems or could create even more intractable policy problems in the future.

The term "information policy" as used here does not suggest that there is or should be a single uniform policy governing all the uses of information systems in both the public and private sectors. In fact, no such policy exists, nor does one appear to be likely.

"Information policy" does suggest the need for consideration of the currently confusing array of laws and regulations—and their strengths, overlaps, contradictions, and deficiencies—within some overall policy issue structure or framework. The structure developed by OTA for use in this and related studies is shown in table 1.

System Issues

The policy issues related to information systems per se focus on their design, implementation, and operation. They generally are concerned with whether the system performs the tasks expected of it with reliability, with appropriate security, and in an efficient and timely manner. These objectives mainly are of interest to the organization operating the system, and place major constraints on the system designer.

Technical, operational, and reliability factors all can have broader societal significance even though they originate in the operational goals of the system itself. In recent years, for example, public attention has been focused on areas such as:

- the safety and reliability of the air traffic control system;

Table 1.—Structure of Information Policy Issues

Level of issues	Character of issues	Example issues
System level	Relate to the design,implementation, and operation of particular information systems.	Government procurement policy. Efficiency and economy of operation. Security of information systems.
Information level	Relate to the handling of data: collection, storage, use, and dissemination.	Privacy (recordkeeping).Freedom of information regulations. Copyright and patents as related to computer programs.
Secondary policy impacts	Exist independent of the particular information systems, but are changed in magnitude or character by use of technology.	Privacy (surveillance). First Amendment rights. Fourth Amendment rights. Social vulnerability. Federal State relations.
Long-term societal effects	Long-range societal impacts that are not currently reflected in specific policy problems, but which may ultimately affect the nature of U.S. society.	Privacy (social attitudes). Psychological self-image of humans. Educational needs. Social-political effects. Cultural impacts.

SOURCE: Office of Technology Assessment, see ch. 5.

*Some recently proposed legislation would establish a comprehensive approach to certain specific problem areas, e.g., privacy and freedom of information. See H.R. 2465, 96th Cong., "Omnibus Right to Privacy Act of 1979." Also the National Telecommunications and Information Administration (NTIA) of the Department of Commerce has made an effort to formulate—or at least to develop a framework for—national information policies. See Arthur A. Bushkin and Jane H. Yurow, *The Foundations of United States Information Policy,* NTIA, Washington, D.C., June 1980, and Jane H. Yurow, et al., *Issues in Information Policy,* Helen A. Shaw (ed.), NTIA, February 1981. See also, Donald A. Dunn, "Information Resources and the New Information Technologies: Implications for Public Policy," National Science Foundation Report to the President and Members of Congress, *The Five-Year Outlook on Science and Technology,* vol. II, May 1980, pp. 493-507.

**The "Paperwork Reduction Act of 1980" (Public Law 96-511) enacted by the 96th Congress does set out a more comprehensive policy and management approach for Federal Government information systems. The Act establishes within the Office of Management and Budget (OMB) an Office of Information and Regulatory Affairs and assigns to that Office a broad range of authorities and required actions.

- the reliability, security, and controllability of military command and control systems, existing and proposed;
- the security of large-scale electronic funds transfer systems; and
- the reliability, accuracy, and responsiveness of the social security information systems.

There is a strong societal interest in the proper and reliable technical operation of each of the systems cited above, and potentially high costs to society if they fail.

Information Issues

The three differing fundamental values of information shown in figure 7 motivate many of the laws and regulations affecting information. Individual regulations or laws usually address only one aspect of information. Policy issues, then, arise from the inherent tensions between the particular values reflected in different laws. Congress is called on to establish balances. These tensions are illustrated below:

- *Public v. private value.* Freedom of information laws (reflecting public value) can conflict with individual or proprietary concerns (reflecting rights to privacy). For example, in serving the public interest, Government collects an extraordinary amount of information about citizens, businesses, and other organizations. Some of this information theoretically has been available to the public by law for a long time but has been protected, in fact, by the amount of effort required to retrieve it from manual recordkeeping systems. Automated systems reduce the cost and time barriers to wider access to these public records, and thereby may accentuate the issue of the extent to which this information can and should be publicly available.
- *Commercial v. public value.* As information becomes a more valuable commercial commodity, increasing tensions are arising between those who wish to sell it through new information systems, and those like the public librarians whose traditional role is to treat information as a public good available to all. These tensions may also stem from the competition between Government-collected data, made available through freedom of information laws, and commercial data services.
- *Commercial v. private value.* Commercially marketable information may invade privacy or proprietary rights, as in the case of computerized mailing lists

Figure 7.—Value Triad of Information: Conflict and Competition Among Private, Commercial, and Public Value

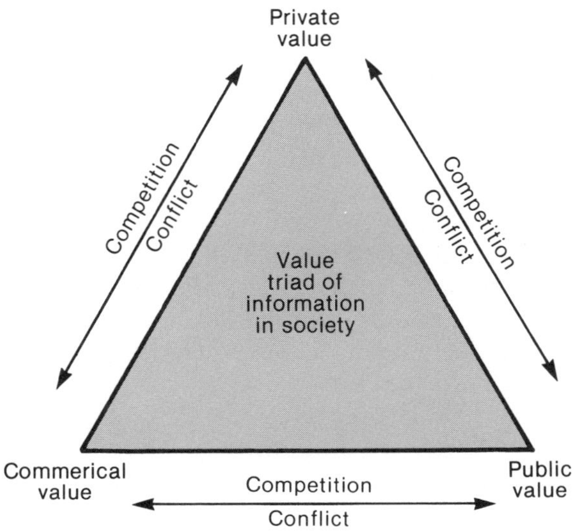

Commercial value of information: Information has been a commodity of commerce for centuries. Books and newspapers, and in this century the broadcasting industry, all sell information. As society becomes more dependent on information, its value increases. The very high growth rate of the computer-based information industry illustrates this trend.

Private value of information: In an information society, economic competition is often based on access to special information, such as a formula for a soft drink, an econometric projection, marketing plans, or geological data. Commercially important information is considered by organizations to be proprietary. Similarly, individuals often consider information about themselves to be private, either because damage can be done by its disclosure or simply because of desiring to be left alone.

Public value of information: American society has always viewed information as having a public value, and has asserted the public interest in a free flow of information. Examples include: the public support of libraries, schools, and museums; a tradition of academic freedom and a system of open scholarly publication; the first amendment guarantees; and freedom of information laws.

SOURCE: Office of Technology Assessment; see ch. 4.

that may be compiled from third-party information sources without the knowledge or consent of the individuals involved.

Secondary Policy Impacts

Computer-based information systems, by increasing the quantity of information collected, the efficiency of its collection and dissemination, its utility, and its ease of storage can cause qualitative changes in the behavior of Government, individuals, and organizations as well as in the nature of traditional conflicts. Thus, the use of automated information systems can have secondary effects on policy problems that have existed for years and in many ways are independent of the technology. Because much more information can be obtained, handled, processed, and distributed so much faster, old problems are not merely exacerbated, but new ones are created.

For example, the increased scale and presumed efficiency of computerized criminal justice recordkeeping intensifies the tension society has always experienced between the needs of law enforcement and the individual rights of citizens. Similarly, the tendency of the technology to encourage centralized record systems creates problems of Federal-State relationships, a particularly touchy issue in law enforcement. Some experts believe this centralization trend could reverse through the use of smaller computers with distributed data bases.

Long-Term Societal Effects

Social scientists engaged in futures studies have suggested that the information revolution, spurred both by advances in computers and communication and by the changing role of information in U.S. society, will have profound long-term effects as dramatic as those caused by the invention of the printing press.

Just as the printing press, by stimulating literacy and speeding the flow of ideas, supported the Renaissance and the transition from medieval society to the age of enlightenment, so the new information systems could profoundly transform the social and political environment of U.S. and world society. Indeed television and sophisticated computer-based polling technology have already had observable effects on the political processes in the United States. Third World leaders calling on UNESCO for a "new world information order" express the belief that information technology will have a central influence on the social and economic development of their countries as well as on international relationships.

This overview study has not attempted to address in detail these broader questions. However, given the potential for significant social change, research funded publicly, privately, or in some jointly developed projects could provide valuable insights into the long-term societal effects of computer-based information systems and related public policy choices.

Public Policy Issues

The overview study examined the national information system issues judged by OTA to be among the most important and likely to warrant congressional attention over the next few years. These issue areas include: innovation, productivity, and employment; privacy; security; Government management of data processing; society's dependence on information systems; constitutional rights; and regulatory and other issues. See chapters 6 through 12 for further discussion.

Innovation, Productivity, and Employment

Innovation, the continual generation of new technological ideas and products and services based on those ideas, is a prime requisite for a healthy industry in a high technology field like computers and information systems. Innovation in information technology improves the productivity of the information industry itself and also offers the tools for improving the productivity of many other sectors of the economy.

Based on anticipated advances in artificial intelligence, robotics, computer control, and input-output technology over the next few years, computer-based factory automation will make a substantial contribution to improving manufacturing productivity. Word processing and other forms of office automation are already improving clerical productivity and may have similar potential for managerial productivity. Intelligent cash registers and automated checkout are directly improving the productivity of retail clerks and indirectly the productivity of retail management (e.g., accounting, inventory control, procurement). The full impact is yet to be felt of these and other applications that are only now starting to be installed in the manufacturing and service sectors of the economy. However, they are likely to help restore an upward trend in the Nation's productivity.

Photo credit: IBM Corp.

The IBM scanner uses holography, a technique for creating three-dimensional images, to read data on packages

From a larger societal perspective, the increased productivity brought about by advances in computer technology may be reflected not only by greater output per employee, but perhaps also in terms of better product quality, improved work environment and job satisfaction, and longer term social benefits such as improved job safety and greater opportunities for on-the-job learning and career advancement.

Congress will be confronted by a number of issues concerned with innovation in computer technology and its effects on productivity and employment:

- *R&D support.* Innovation in computer and information technology depends on continued, aggressive R&D. Many U.S. corporations in the information industry, realizing that their success depends on continued innovation, have established their own research centers. Several Federal agencies* support computer R&D, although the major part of development support comes from the Department of Defense and related agencies. An important issue is whether research in the applications of computer technology to problems in the private (civilian) sector—in such areas as education,** health, transportation, environmental quality, and job safety—is receiving adequate Federal support, given the critical nature of computer technology to the Nation's well-being.
- *Vitality of academic computer science.* Basic research in computer science is largely carried out in universities. Because of the close connection between applied technology and basic research, the vitality of the computer industry is in part dependent on the vitality of academic computer science. However, university departments of computer sciences are experiencing problems in ob-

*Including the National Science Foundation, National Aeronautics and Space Administration, and Department of Energy.

**Information Technology and Education is the subject of another OTA assessment in progress.

taining the faculty, facilities, and funds needed to do the research and to train new experts. This situation is particularly critical in systems design and software engineering.

- *Impacts on employment.* It is still uncertain whether the productivity increases brought about by computer technology will increase or decrease the overall employment level. Structural shifts in the economy are likely to occur since any innovation which creates new products and new industries will eliminate some jobs only to create others. Even if new jobs are created or old ones redefined, not all workers will find it easy or desirable to shift. Some employees may be unwilling or unable to adapt themselves to the new technology or may be untrainable in the new procedures.
- *Support for computer impact research.* The area of employment impacts is a good example of the need for computer impact research, a new field developed over the last decade by computer and social scientists. To date, however, university groups and others have experienced difficulty in securing financial support, in part because this subject does not fit comfortably into traditional scientific research programs. Computer impact research is not pure computer science; neither is it classifiable as purely social or political science. The results of such research could supply valuable input to the kinds of public policy issues identified in this overview study.
- *International competitiveness.* Computer and communication technologies are moving ahead so rapidly that products can become obsolete within a few years. Although the United States holds a substantial positive balance of trade (and employment) in certain areas of information technology, the maintenance of this balance depends in part on continued R&D and innovation and on supportive public policies.* Because of aggressive import competition from Europe, Japan, and Canada, even domestic markets are vulnerable to any faltering in the technological lead.

Privacy

Privacy-related issues dealing with the collection, dissemination, and use of personal information are likely to remain on the congressional agenda for a number of reasons:

- *An omnibus v. a selective privacy policy.* The Federal Government has deliberately chosen up to now to react to privacy issues associated with recordkeeping on a case-by-case basis rather than through omnibus legislation, which would cover all data systems both public and private in which personal information is maintained.

  With the selective approach, Congress will be considering a long series of privacy bills. To catch up with current computerized recordkeeping practices will require a substantial legislative effort. An immediate concern is to develop privacy rules for computer applications in banking, medicine, social and medical research, credit, insurance, and criminal justice. Privacy is also likely to be a major issue in the development of electronic mail.

  Congress may need to consider alternative approaches to privacy policy.
- *New technologies, new problems.* New applications for computer and communication technology, such as an automated securities exchange, in-home information services, electronic publishing, and the automated office, may create new environments for privacy

*Relevant policy instruments include taxation, antitrust, and standards, among others. U.S. industrial competitiveness in the international electronics and computer markets is the subject of another OTA assessment in progress.

policy issues to arise. As Government agencies such as the Department of Justice, IRS, or the Social Security Administration begin to use the latest generation of information technology for their recordkeeping activities, privacy problems that were not specifically addressed in previous legislation may have to be dealt with by Congress.

- *Secondary use of personal information.* A fundamental assumption underlying much of the privacy debate in the 1970's was that collecting personal information is in the nature of a transaction—the individual yields personal information in exchange for some benefit. Thus, much of the fair practice doctrine centers on the requirement that the recordkeeper abide by obligations implicit in that transaction. However, individuals will increasingly be encountering computerized systems that collect and store information about them without their knowledge or consent. Very little law exists pertaining to the ownership or disposition of such information, even when its use may be contrary to the individual's perception of his or her interests.
- *Microprocessors and surveillance.* The potential now exists for the development and marketing of a wide variety of microprocessor and computer/communication devices either specifically designed or capable of being used for the surveillance of individuals without their consent. Microprocessor-based locks can provide detailed records of the whereabouts of anyone in a building. Devices called "pen registers" provide a similar capability for monitoring telephone traffic. Abuse of this technology for illicit purposes may become a serious problem. Even seemingly legitimate applications (e.g., employer monitoring of employee phone calls to deter nonwork-related conversations) may, if abused, raise in new forms the classic issues of civil rights versus both law enforcement and the rights of employers to monitor their employees.

Security

The technology for securing computer systems from theft, sabotage, natural hazards, and the like is improving steadily, and users are becoming more aware of the need to protect information. However, the increasingly complicated computer-based information systems being designed and built make secure operation more and more difficult.

Among the several difficult issues involving computer security that are likely to confront Congress, the following appear to be the most significant:

- *Protection of Federal systems.* Federal information systems control the disbursement of an enormous amount of money. The Social Security system itself disburses over $2 billion per week. Other Federal systems contain information that could be used directly or indirectly to make profitable financial decisions, e.g., information on Federal monetary policy, on commodity markets, and on energy resource estimates. Still others contain sensitive information relating to personal privacy or national security. All would be highly attractive to theft, manipulation, or eavesdropping.

  These are not the only threats to Federal computer systems that Congress will need to consider. A more subtle threat is a system's potential diversion by the bureaucracy from its intended use; for example, the use of computerized criminal histories for employment or licensing purposes. As the Government continues to automate, problems of bureaucratic accountability and the responsibility for oversight will confront Congress with the need to better understand and more closely monitor the use of large Federal information systems.

- *Protection of vital domestic information systems.* There is a Federal responsibility for certain information systems that, although privately operated, are fundamental to social well-being. The security and reliability of automated systems for nationwide bank check clearing, electronic message systems, and computer-based commodity trading, for example, would all be under the purview of Congress. The vulnerability of such systems is of governmental concern because of the harm that a major system failure could cause to the Nation's economy and to its citizens.
- *Development of data security and cryptographic capability.* The Federal Government, due to its traditional concern for the protection of military and diplomatic communications, has a high degree of expertise in the field of data security. For example, the National Bureau of Standards is developing computer security guidelines and standards for use by Federal agencies. The first standard to emerge from this effort is the Data Encryption* Standard (DES) for protecting data communication.

  While the DES is public, much of the Federal expertise is either classified or in the hands of highly sensitive organizations such as the National Security Agency. The appropriate role of the Federal Government has not been defined in transferring this knowledge, supporting computer security research in both the public and private sectors, setting standards for non-Federal systems, and certifying security technology.

  The lack of such policy definition is visible in the current debate over Government control of cryptographic technology. In this debate, the needs of the private sector for increased communication security, and hence for the existence of a civilian commercial cryptographic capability, are set against the perceptions of the defense community that such development threatens national security concerns by putting sensitive information in the public domain. A related issue is the desire in the academic community for the freedom to conduct research on the mathematics underlying cryptography.

*Encryption is the coding of a message so that it is only understandable to a receiver who knows the secret decoding procedure and/or key.

Government Management of Data Processing

In the early days of computing, the Federal Government as a user was a principal stimulus to the development of the field. Although a few instances of Federal expertise at the leading edge of computer applications remain, the Federal Government is rapidly falling behind the private sector in its use and management of up-to-date computer and information technology. Such a lag would penalize Government operations in two ways:

1. potentially lost opportunities to use the newest technology to improve the efficiency and effectiveness of Government programs; and
2. increased cost and decreased reliability resulting from operating systems that are becoming obsolete, from archaic management procedures, and from burdensome procurement restrictions.

Cheaper computing hardware, the emergence of data communication-based systems, and new software techniques are changing the way computers are used in industry. The next 10 years will see significant movement in the private sector toward automating the flow of information in offices, toward experimenting with new management structures based on high-volume data communication, and toward automating decision support systems for use by higher management. To the extent that these applications fulfill their promise of improvement in both the quality and productivity of management, the Federal Government would be remiss in not making use of them where appropriate.

The most recent legislative action to address this problem is Public Law 96-511, known as the Paperwork Reduction Act of 1980, which establishes central oversight in the Office of Management and Budget of the information policies and practices of the executive branch. Perhaps most important, this Act emphasizes the basic need for restructuring the way information resources and supporting technologies are managed in the Government. This represents a new and as yet untested approach by giving management of information resources similar importance to that traditionally assigned to managing financial and personnel resources.

Many other issues and questions also need attention from this broader perspective. For example:

- *Automated bureaucracy.* There is a need to better understand the effects of large-scale information systems on the internal organization and management of Government agencies and on Federal decisionmaking. What effects do these systems have on the location of responsibility, the quality of the decisions, the nature of due process for clients affected by those decisions, and the accountability of the bureaucracy to higher-level policymakers in the executive branch and to Congress itself?
- *Social values and goals.* The process by which appropriate social values and goals are reflected in Federal information systems design needs clarification. Major new systems will need to be evaluated for their effects on privacy, security, constitutional rights, and many other issues that are not normally the concern of the designer or operator of an information system.

  Three fundamental approaches are available to deal with social value questions:

  1. Congress could assess the potential social impacts of each new system design that is proposed on a case-by-case basis.
  2. Congress could codify a social impact policy concerning all Federal information processing systems. An appropriate agency could be designated as responsible for seeing that all new system designs are evaluated in relation to that policy.
  3. Congress could continue to examine agency proposals system by system, but would base its evaluation on a social impact framework encompassing a set of principles for the design and operation of Federal information systems.

Whatever the approach, it will be necessary for Congress to balance the need to speed up design and procurement of Federal systems, against the requirements that tax money be spent as effectively and as equitably as possible and the necessity to consider carefully the societal impacts of these systems.

Society's Dependence on Information Systems

The nature of risk is being changed by much of the new high technology on which modern society depends—jumbo commercial airlines, nuclear powerplants, oil supertankers, or large computer-based information systems. In general, because new technologies can be designed to operate more reliably than the ones replaced, the risk that any particular mechanism may fail has been reduced. However, should an accidental or deliberate disruption occur, its cost can be much larger, even catastrophic. Furthermore, when society becomes highly dependent on the reliable functioning of a single integrated technological system or small collection of such systems, the possibility of a "domino-like" collapse of several of the individual connected units could also be disastrous.

This evolution to dependency can be seen already in the reliance of safe public air transport on the continuous operation of the computerized air traffic control system.* In the commercial sector, large stores and banks rely on the smooth uninterrupted operation of their computer systems.

Thus, as society moves toward electronic funds transfer systems, widely available electronic mail service, and other large extensively used information systems, the following factors warrant consideration:

- The ways in which public policy can help to allocate and balance the risks society may encounter from national information systems against the benefits it may receive, under conditions where failure rates appear to be low but potential losses may be high should a failure occur.
- The ability of society to retain the option to end its dependence on a particular information system if it has unanticipated undesirable effects; in other words, to avoid the possibility of becoming "locked in" to the use of certain information systems once they are installed.
- The capability of providing alternatives to persons or institutions choosing not to accept perceived risks in a new information system.
- The ways in which technology can be utilized to reduce the risks, for example by introducing additional system redundancy (alternative paths between points in the system, distributed data bases, backup computers). The risks inherent in U.S. dependence on a nationwide, interconnected telephone system (which itself is rapidly being computerized) are minimized by the large number of circuit switching centers and parallel trunklines.

Large complex information systems contain millions of logical connections and are controlled by programs that themselves can be composed of millions of instructions. Consequently, it is difficult to calculate their reliability and to predict the failure rate of any particular part of the system, as well as the effect of a failure on the operation of the entire system. New research in risk analysis is needed to address the problem of estimating risks under these conditions.

*The airport and air traffic control system is the subject of another OTA assessment.

Constitutional Rights

Little legal precedent exists, in many cases, for applying constitutional law to the issues raised by computer-based information systems. This overview study identified several areas of constitutional rights that may be affected by information systems, as illustrated below:

The *first amendment* guarantees freedom of religion, speech, the press, peaceable assembly, and the right to petition for redress of grievances.

- A principal first amendment issue facing the Government may be how to encourage the maximum freedom of expression—fostering the "marketplace of ideas"—in new electronic media that have been tightly regulated in more traditional forms. For example, the scarcity of frequency spectrum and channel capacity that provided a basis for regulation of broadcast television may not apply to new versions of TV such as cable, direct-to-home satellite, and videotext.
- Another first amendment issue may be generated by extensive data collection and possibly surveillance by Government and private organizations that could, in fact, suppress or "chill" freedoms of speech, assembly, and even religion by the implicit threats contained in such collection or surveillance. These threats might be directed as much at the "listener" as the "speaker." Clearly, automated information delivery systems possess a much greater capability for recording, storing, and analyzing in detail the flow of information from all sources into homes and offices, than do manual systems

such as bookstores, newspapers, and the like.

The *fourth amendment* protects the persons, houses, papers, and effects of individuals against unreasonable searches and seizures by the Federal Government.

- Fourth amendment issues may develop from:
  - —the use of personal and statistical data contained in automated information systems as a justification for search and seizure;
  - —the search and seizure of information per se as personal property, particularly in electronic form; and
  - —the use of automated information systems as a tool for search and seizure operations.

An electronic mail cover illustrates the latter type of fourth amendment issue. A nonelectronic mail cover requires approval by the Postal Inspection Service but not a search warrant because only the outside of an envelope is examined. In an electronic mail system, however, no distinction may exist between the "outside" (or address) and the "inside" (or contents) of a message. Therefore, it may be difficult to distinguish a mail cover from a wiretap, which would require a warrant issued by a court upon probable cause, unless some form of coding was used to "seal" an electronic message as an envelope seals a physical one.

The *fifth amendment* guarantees that a person may not be compelled to be a witness against himself or be deprived of life, liberty, or property without due process of law.

- A fifth amendment issue could arise from the use of personal or corporate computer data that have been collected by the Government for one purpose as evidentiary material in unrelated criminal or regulatory cases.
- Another fifth amendment issue could develop from the delivery of Government services by computer-based information systems. For example, very large systems that "mass produce" decisions in such areas as health benefits, student loans, or tax returns may have subtle biases "built in" to the program or code of the computer. These systems may react quickly to what the computer recognizes as "normal" applications, but reject "unusual" claims. If, as a consequence, citizens are subjected to an unacceptable amount of hassle, delay and/or error, the program or code used by the computer to define "normal" or the entire information system may become subject to due process challenge.

The *sixth amendment* guarantees, among other things, the right of a speedy and public trial by an impartial jury.

- A sixth amendment issue may be raised by the growing use of computerized dossiers of potential jurors along with computer models for predicting juror behavior. At this time, computer-based jury selection is very expensive and its value is controversial. However, future computer technology and social scientific techniques may make this application cheap and improve its effectiveness. If so, the entire concept of an "impartial" jury may be challenged.

The *14th amendment* guarantees that a State cannot deprive any person of life, liberty, or property without due process of law nor deny any person within its jurisdiction the equal protection of the laws.

- Fifth and 14th amendment issues may develop from a similar application of computer-based social science and statistical models to predicting criminal behavior and to aid in such tasks as approving credit, determining insurability, or hiring and promoting employees. Essentially, individuals may be denied rights, privileges, and benefits based, not on past performance, but on a prediction of future tendencies. For example, society cannot imprison a person that a computer model predicts may someday rob a bank. But should that knowledge be "probable cause" to monitor such a person closely or deny employment?

Regulatory Boundaries

As computer-based information systems evolve, they challenge traditional concepts of boundaries—physical or social—that are reflected in the law and regulatory policy. The integration of computer and communication technologies creates systems that cross boundaries between nations, States, and organizations. The issue of transborder data flow discussed in chapter 12 exemplifies the kinds of international problems created. Others include the following:

- *Interstate conflict of laws:* When States have conflicting laws involving information or information processing, for example, property laws that cover computer data bases, an integrated data system that exists in a number of different States can raise difficult questions of legal jurisdiction.
- *Federalism:* Linking Federal data systems with State and local systems complicates problems even further. Issues of federalism could arise with systems containing data on criminal history, taxation, welfare, education, medical care, and drug abuse, among others.
- *Antitrust:* Policy issues may arise with respect to whether large integrated data systems using shared facilities create monopolistic barriers to new entrants or are mechanisms for control of the market, or whether they encourage competition by reducing the cost of access for smaller firms.

Information technology is changing form so fast that it is tending to outstrip the working definitions of devices and services that serve as the basis for law and regulation. These definitional problems relate both to the technology itself, and to the products and services that depend on it.

- *Computers or communication:* The best known example is the continuing attempt by the Federal Communications Commission to establish what services and what technologies are already "communications," thus regulated, and what are "computer" services and technologies, thus not regulatable. Their second inquiry on these questions, which began in 1976, only recently resulted in an opinion that is now under court challenge. Even if the definition is accepted, there is no reason to believe that the problem has been permanently resolved.
- *Branch banking:* Many States have laws that either prohibit or tightly regulate branch banks. An issue that has been widely debated is whether the automated extensions of banking (e.g., automatic teller machines or pay-by-phone services) constitute "branches" in the usual meaning of the law.
- *The status of electronic mail:* Electronic data transmission has opened a major policy question about the definition of mail. As with the computer/communication issue above, this definition is significant because it places a class of services under one or another set of regulations. Unlike many other countries that have combined postal and telecommunication services under one national agency, the United States has pursued completely different approaches to regulating each service category. Electronic mail, in its various forms, provides a new service with features of both manual delivery and telecommunication, and may pose new and difficult regulatory questions.

Other Issues

Four other issue areas were identified as important although not analyzed in great detail:

1. *Computer crime:* Crime directed against computer-based information systems or in which these systems are used as tools for criminal activity.

2. *Transborder data flow:* Problems that arise from differing national attitudes and laws regarding the increasing flow of data and interconnection of information systems across national boundaries.
3. *Information gap:* The possibility that some individuals or groups would be denied access to information services vital to their survival in an information society because of technological illiteracy, lack of economic resources, or other reasons.
4. *Computer software protection:* The concern that continuing uncertainty about copyright and patent protection for computer software is significantly impairing software R&D and innovation.

Chapter 2
Background and Purpose of the Study

Contents

LIST OF TABLES

Chapter 2
Background and Purpose of the Study

Introduction

As computer-based national information systems become more important to American society, particularly for Government administration, they create corresponding public policy problems. Thus, over the past 10 to 15 years Congress has been confronted with a series of increasingly complex issues growing out of the way computer-based systems have been designed and used. These have covered a wide range of concerns such as:

- the design, procurement, and operation of Government data systems;
- the potential for Government agencies to abuse the large record systems they operate that contain personal data;
- the effects of computer technology on the structure and operations of the banking industry;
- the role of the Postal Service in providing electronic message service;
- problems concerned with the protection of privacy and constitutional rights presented by the use of large automated data systems; and
- the impact of information technologies on copyright laws.

Congressional and public interest in these and related issues has been illustrated by a variety of actions over the last decade.

- New legislation—bills and acts concerning privacy, standards, and computer crime.
- Special commissions—the Privacy Protection Study Commission, the Commission on Electronic Funds Transfer, the Commission on Postal Service, and the Commission on New Technological Uses of Copyrighted Works.
- Hearings on privacy, Government recordkeeping practices, the impacts of particular Government systems, constitutional rights, innovation in the microelectronics industry, the use of computers in education, and many other topics.
- Regulatory and interagency jurisdictional issues—such as protracted computer regulation inquiries by the Federal Communications Commission (FCC), and challenges to regulatory authorities involving the FCC and the Postal Rate Commission.
- Studies—requests by the legislative branch to the Office of Technology Assessment (OTA), the Congressional Research Service (CRS), and the General Accounting Office (GAO) for studies on particular issues involving information systems. These parallel extensive similar activities in both the executive and judicial branches.

Executive branch interest is illustrated by the formation of the National Telecommunications and Information Administration (NTIA) in the Department of Commerce, by research projects on computer and telecommunication impacts funded by the National Science Foundation, and by a variety of executive orders regarding Federal data processing practices. Interagency groups have been formed to address domestic and international information policy and planning problems.

This overview is one of a group of four studies collectively entitled "Assessment of Societal Impacts of National Information Systems." The individual studies are:

- an overview assessment of technology and public policy issues relevant to computer-based national information systems;

- an assessment of the National Crime Information Center (NCIC) and Computerized Criminal History (CCH) Systems;
- a preliminary assessment of the role of the U.S. Postal Service in electronic message systems; and
- a preliminary assessment of electronic funds transfer systems.

This overview report is intended to be a broad introductory examination of computer-based national information systems and related technology and public policy issues that Congress is likely to face over the next few years. It will also serve as a foundation for the other three OTA studies and for future in-depth examination of particular systems and issues. It should also generate an awareness of the increasingly critical role that national information systems play in society.

Congressional Requests

Over the last 5 years, OTA has received a number of requests from congressional committees and subcommittees to study and report on the impacts of national information systems on society and on public policy.

TAS and NCIC: In February 1976, the House Ways and Means Committee and its Subcommittee on Oversight requested that OTA conduct an assessment of the new Tax Administration System (TAS) proposed by the Internal Revenue Service. In September 1976, the Subcommittee on Government Information and Individual Rights of the House Government Operations Committee also requested such a study in a letter that raised, in addition, much broader questions about Government information systems. Both requests stressed the issues of privacy and the impact of TAS on the Government's use of tax return information.

In September 1977, the House Judiciary Committee, together with its Subcommittee on Civil and Constitutional Rights, requested an assessment of NCIC administered by the Federal Bureau of Investigation. The requests expressed particular concern with the CCH Program and its possible detrimental effects on privacy and civil liberties.

In response to these requests, OTA carried out preliminary assessments of both systems. The TAS preliminary assessment was published in March 1977[1] and the NCIC preliminary assessment in December 1978.[2]

Additional Requests: Subsequently, OTA received a number of congressional letters endorsing these assessments but also raising broader questions concerned with information policy. Some were directed at specific categories of systems under a particular committee's jurisdiction; others dealt more generally with social impacts in areas such as privacy and constitutional rights. The concerns expressed in the requests spanned a number of different applications in both the private sector and the Federal Government. A number of these requests and their particular areas of interest are shown in table 2.

In July 1980, a letter was sent to OTA by Cong. George E. Brown, a member of the Technology Assessment Board and then Chairman of the Subcommittee on Science, Research, and Technology of the House Science and Technology Committee. It expressed an even broader and more compre-

[1]U.S. Congress, Office of Technology Assessment, *A Preliminary Analysis of the IRS Tax Administration System, OTA-TCI-43,* March 1977.

[2]U.S. Congress, Office of Technology Assessment, *A Preliminary Assessment of the National Crime Information Center and the Computerized Criminal History System, OTA-I-80,* December 1978.

Table 2.—Summary of Congressional Requests for OTA Assessments Concerning National Information Systems

Date	Committee or subcommittee	Areas of interest
February 1977	House Committee on Post Office and Civil Service	Requested an assessment of electronic mail, emphasizing the role of the U.S. Postal Service and employment impacts.
September 1977	House Subcommittee on Government Information and Individual Rights (of the House Committee on Government Operations)	Reaffirmed a previous request for a TAS study and encouraged a wider look at the impact of Government information systems on privacy, freedom of information, and other related issues, and asked OTA to explore a possible Government-wide policy on data systems.
September 1977	House Subcommittee on Civil and Constitutional Rights (House Committee on the Judiciary)	Requested a full assessment of NCIC.
January-June 1978	Senate Committee on the Judiciary; Subcommittee on Administrative Practice and Procedure; Subcommittee on the Constitution	Requested a full assessment of NCIC. Raised issues of constitutional rights, privacy, other civil liberty concerns, and Federalism.
December 1978	Senate Committee on the Judiciary; Subcommittee on Administrative Practice and Procedure; Subcommittee on Antitrust and Monopoly; Subcommittee on the Constitution; Subcommittee on Criminal Law and Procedure	Requested a study of the impact of telecommunications and domestic information systems on constitutional rights, civil liberties, privacy, freedom of information, antitrust and constitutional rights. Requested NCIC study. Specifically mentioned electronic banking applications, electronic mail, and criminal justice systems.

SOURCE: Office of Technology Assessment.

hensive range of concerns about the societal impacts of information technology. Congressman Brown requested that, given the breadth and complexity of the subject, OTA undertake a preliminary study to create a "map" of the field. This map would include the major technologies, their areas of application, the impact issues, and the principal current efforts by various agencies to study these problems.

OTA Response

In October 1978, the national information systems (NIS) assessment was initiated by OTA, following a March 1978 approval by the Technology Assessment Board. It was designed with four components:

- an assessment of NCIC/CCH;
- an assessment of the role of the U.S. Postal Service in electronic message systems;
- an assessment of electronic funds transfer systems; and
- an overview of the crosscutting impacts of all information systems.

These were at first envisaged as case study components in a single large assessment of the impacts of national information systems. In time, however, they evolved into separate studies. The basis for this modification was the following judgment, which was confirmed by the OTA Advisory Panel on National Information Systems and the OTA staff.

While some observations can be made about national information systems in general, full assessments of their policy impacts can only be made in the context of particular systems, particular applications, and/or particular users, and legal/social environments.

Consequently, each case study needed to be carried out as an individual assessment in which the characteristic issues raised by that type of system would be addressed in its own legal, regulatory, social, and economic environment. It was questionable, however, whether the overview study would be effective as a unifying effort cutting across the three other studies by generalizing their results. Thus, its goals had to be carefully examined and clarified.

In addition, in late 1978, in response to requests from the House and Senate Committees concerned with communication policy, an assessment of telecommunication systems was begun at OTA and conducted in parallel with the NIS assessment. The telecommunication study focused on an examination of common carrier policy and impacts.[3] Both assessments have been closely coordinated to avoid duplication of effort particularly in the analyses of industry structure and technology.

[3]U.S. Congress, Office of Technology Assessment, *Telecommunication Technology and Public Policy.*

NIS Study Goals

It would not be possible for any one study to capture succinctly a single set of policy issues which would apply to all national information systems in American society. The specific systems applications are too different, the potentials and problems too complex, and the parties-at-interest and relevant institutional and legal framework too diverse.

Faced with a complexity of possible topics, OTA established the following set of limited goals for this overview study:

- *To provide a general introduction to computer-based national information systems:* This study should acquaint the nonexpert reader with the nature of computer-based national information systems, their roles in American society, and the characteristics of their impacts and the policy issues that result from their use.
- *To provide a foundation and context for the other related OTA assessments:* The NCIC/CCH, electronic funds transfer, and electronic message system studies all require fundamental state-of-the-art surveys of the computer and related technologies and industries. This data base is provided by the overview report. In addition, a framework of potential impacts is laid out within which the specific issues raised in each study can be explored.
- *To build a foundation for future studies:* Over the next few years, Congress will continually be confronted with a number of issues loosely characterized as being related to "information policy." Congressional agencies such as OTA, CRS, and GAO, as well as executive branch agencies such as NTIA, are being asked to address these issues.

To date, most research and writing about the impacts of computerized information systems have been unrelated. Different terminology, different concepts about the nature of the impacts, and different analytic methodologies have been used. There is a need for some consistent structure, such as a map of the information technology field as discussed by Congressman Brown in his letter to OTA. A start is made toward developing such an analytic framework in chapter 5.

This study's assessment of the directions the development of computer technology and its applications to national information systems will take provides a useful baseline for future work. The description of the current status of the information industry and its likely evolution will be useful in projecting possible future services and the nature of the market and regulatory forces that may shape those services.

Study Methodology

The limited nature of this study's goals, along with its role of providing a supporting framework for the three other studies, dictated a modest plan using in-house staff supplemented by an advisory panel and other ad hoc expert review. The project was organized around the following information-gathering tasks:

- technology,
- industry structure,
- social trends,
- legal and regulatory environment, and
- policy issues analysis.

Technology: This survey examines the current state of computer technology and projects its development over the next 10 to 20 years. It stresses the technology likely to be available to computer users, rather than the leading-edge capabilities likely to exist only in laboratories and on drawing boards. A working paper prepared by OTA staff was reviewed by a special technology panel set up for that purpose. This was coordinated with a parallel effort supporting the telecommunication assessment. The technology survey is highlighted in chapter 3, presented in detail in chapter 13, and used throughout the report.

Industry Structure: This survey examines the current state of the computer and information industries, describes growth trends, and projects their development over the next decade. It, too, was an in-house staff effort, drawing on the technology panel for review and input, and coordinated with the telecommunication assessment. The survey of industry structure and the technology are highlighted in chapter 3, presented in detail in chapter 14, and likewise used throughout the report.

Social Trends: A small task was undertaken to list those political, economic, and social trends believed likely either to have an impact on the use of computer-based information systems or to be affected by their application. A brief working paper was drafted, reviewed by an ad hoc workshop of outside experts, revised in accordance with their comments, and integrated into chapter 4 and the policy issue chapters (6 through 12).

Legal and Regulatory Environment: The in-house staff examined the range of legal and regulatory requirements, existing or pending, that affect the use of computer-based information systems. Analyses were prepared in 13 areas of law and regulation. These were reviewed for accuracy and completeness by a pro bono mail review panel of legal experts, and then utilized in chapter 5 and in the policy issue chapters.

Policy Issues Analysis: An initial list of issues was prepared by OTA staff (see table 3). It was later modified by consideration of the following:

- concerns mentioned in the congressional requests;
- panel advice on priorities;
- comparison with issues examined in the NCIC/CCH, electronic funds transfer, and electronic mail studies;
- comparison with issues developed in the parallel telecommunication study; and
- possible and likely future studies by OTA in related areas.

The topics selected for further analysis do not represent a complete list of all the principal national information system issues that may confront Congress over the next decade. In OTA's judgment, however, these will be among the most important. The brief essays presented in chapters 6 through 12 are not intended as full analyses of these issues. Rather, they describe the general nature of the conflicts, and how future applications of computer-based information systems may intensify or alter the character of the policy debate and the need for new laws and policies.

Table 3.—Initial Working List of Impact and Issue Areas[a]

Economic impacts and issues
1. Costs, economic growth, and availability of services
2. Technological displacement, obsolescence, and impact on the work force
3. Resource availability and demand
4. Competition
5. Regulation and standards
6. Research and development (innovation in both hardware and software services)
7. Public goods
8. International markets and services
9. Effects on other industries (e.g., travel)
10. Employee rights and privileges and labor-management relations

Social impacts and issues
1. Privacy
2. Confidentiality
3. Security
4. Due process and fairness (individual access, accuracy, timeliness, currency, and purging)
5. Freedom of information
6. Equity, social justice, and equality of access to services
7. Civil liberties (first, fourth, and fifth amendments)—constitutional rights
8. Surveillance and social control
9. Changes in the basic social structure and functioning of groups (e.g., families), organizations (e.g., schools), and institutions (e.g., banking)
10. Centralization and decentralization
11. Educational changes
12. Public participation
13. Accountability and oversight

Legal Impacts and Issues
1. Copyrights, patents, trade secrets, and ownership of information
2. Antitrust

Political impacts and issues
1. Federalism and intergovernmental relations
2. International sovereignty
3. National security

[a]It is recognized that several topics fall under more than one group heading, however, they were not listed more than once; e.g. certain social impacts and issues could also be shown under legal impacts and issues and/or under political impacts and issues.

SOURCE: Office of Technology Assessment.

Chapter 3
Information Systems and Computers

Contents

Chapter 3
Information Systems and Computers

The Nature of Computer-Based Information Systems

Traditionally, the popular view of computers has been that they are super calculators that automate processes which were previously performed by numbers of people sitting at mechanical adding machines. However, computers carry out a wide variety of tasks associated with processing information. It is important to understand the entire range of these capabilities in order to appreciate the nature and magnitude of the potential social impacts of this technology when used in information systems.

Computer capabilities fall into seven main categories:

1. *Data collection.* When attached to various sensing devices, computers can detect and measure such external physical phenomena as temperature, time, pressure, flow rate, consumption rate, or any number of other variables. Also, computers can keep a record of transactions. For example, a computerized cash register can collect and store information about a sale that includes bookkeeping entries, taxes, commissions and inventory, and can even reorder stock. Some computer-based door locks require individuals to carry magnetic identity cards. Such locks not only can control access but also can create a record of whose card was granted access, when, and for how long.

   Technological advances are beginning to provide computers with the capability to directly process visual and audio input, thus greatly increasing their applicability to data collection. Computers already have a limited ability to recognize human speech, to read directly a variety of typewritten forms and handprinted texts, and to detect patterns in video images. These functions will be improving rapidly over the next decade and will appear in commercial equipment.
2. *Information storage.* Computers can store large amounts of information for long periods of time in an electronic-readable form that is easily and quickly recoverable. Depending on the particular application, the methods of storage vary widely, from signals in electronic circuitry, to magnetic pulses on tape, to holes in cards. New advances in memory technology eventually will allow trillions of characters of information to be stored conveniently and cheaply wherever there is even a small computer. The cost of storing information electronically will soon be substantially lower than the cost of storing the same amount of information on paper.
3. *Information organization.* Computers can be used to rearrange information so that it is more suitable for particular applications. For example, if the data in a telephone directory were stored in a computer's memory, it could be inverted to allow one to look up a telephone number that corresponds to a particular address. More generally, computers can simplify and restructure vast amounts of raw data to assist people in drawing significant meanings or conclusions.
4. *Calculations.* Computers perform arithmetic calculations millions of times faster than can human beings. They are used to make numerous simple calculations, such as those required in processing the payroll for a sizable organization; to make sophisticated statistical calculations on large amounts of data,

such as those for social science research; or to perform highly complex scientific calculations, such as those needed for weather research or for modeling fusion energy systems.

5. *Communication.* Through connections over a telecommunication system, computers can transmit data around the Nation and the world either to human users or to other computers, which permits the sharing of work and data among groups of linked computers (known as computer networking). Private firms are beginning to offer special communication services to support computer networking. In addition, computers make possible the more effective use and management of the communication systems themselves.
6. *Information presentation.* Computers can put out information in a variety of forms. Through graphical display, and more recently through voice response, they can make data readily understandable and useful to nonexperts. It is possible to have data and computer schematics displayed on screens in a multicolored, three-dimensional format for design and analytical purposes. Also, data such as numbers and statistics can be organized by the computer in an easy-to-understand tabular presentation. Much of the programing effort in developing modern management information systems is directed toward designing ways in which the information generated by the computer can be presented most clearly to the manager who needs it.
7. *Control.* Computers can be used to control a machine tool or a production line without human intervention. Many consumer devices—including microwave ovens, automated home thermostats, automobile engines, television sets, and telephones—incorporate computer controls using new microprocessor technology. Such uses are increasing rapidly.

Several of these capabilities can be combined, for example in *computer-aided design* of aircraft structures (or computer logic elements, for that matter) and *computer-based modeling* of the saltwater penetration in San Francisco Bay (a function of tidal action and ground water runoff). Both computer-aided design and computer modeling are finding wide application and are illustrative of what is sometimes referred to as the "intelligence amplifying" capability of computers.

History of Computer Use

Over the last 30 years, computer systems have evolved through stages that emphasized particular capabilities and that have altered the way society handles information. The nature of these applications has been shaped, in part, by the available technology, but also by the changing perception of computers and how they may be used most effectively.

Few applications were new, however, at least in the beginning. Society has kept records and exchanged information for centuries. It is important to understand this background, since many computer impacts, both beneficial and adverse, arise from the changes in historical information practices that occur when computer systems are substituted for manual systems.

Some significant trends in the development of computer applications are discussed below:

Computer trends in the 1950's: Increased size and centralization.

In the 1950's, every announcement of a new, larger computer elicited the comment that only a few would be needed to serve the computer needs of the entire country. "Grosch's Law"—an empirical estimate that one could get four times the computing power at twice the cost—provided an economy-of-scale rationale for large, centralized systems.

This underlying economic rationale forced organizations to pool their computing applications in central computer centers that would run them on as large a machine as possible. This operating style, which can still be seen in many organizations, had two principal drawbacks.

One effect, seen immediately, was that centralization separated the users from the computer forcing them to gain access to the machine through layers of bureaucracy. Some applications were not harmed in such an environment. However, delays and bureaucratic costs inhibited the work of such users as scientists, engineers, and students. They often could not perform the type of creative work that the computer was expected to foster.

The second effect was more subtle. Economy-of-scale no doubt existed technologically—multiplying two numbers was cheaper on a larger machine. However, designers had to generalize the computer hardware and programs in order to handle all of the different types of applications that had been pooled to justify the big machines. Thus, preparing a payroll, performing small engineering computations, and calculating a very complicated mathematical model, all might be handled by the same computer. Some of the theoretical efficiency gain for a large general-purpose computer was lost in the system overhead required to provide the facility for such a variety of applications.

Despite these drawbacks, computer use grew rapidly during this period. Most applications concentrated on using computers both as calculators and as controllers of large (for that time) record systems, usually kept on magnetic tapes or punched cards.

Computer trends in the 1960's: The minicomputer and timesharing.

In the 1960's, motivated by the two above-mentioned drawbacks, users on university campuses and in research laboratories developed two design concepts that fundamentally altered the way in which computers would be used—the minicomputer and timesharing.

In the early years, many scientists learned about using computers by sitting at them and programing them directly. Chafing at the bureaucratic and physical barriers being erected around the central system, these users developed small, specialized laboratory computers which, although not cheap by current standards, were far less expensive than the centralized systems that often cost in excess of a million dollars. These small machines, or minicomputers, were cheap enough so that a person sitting and working at one could afford to use it at less than optimum efficiency. The loss of machine efficiency was offset by the increase in human efficiency.

The other important concept, "timesharing," was developed because a large system cost hundreds of dollars per minute to operate. Thus, an individual could not engage in a rewarding working session sitting directly at a large computer, which was dedicated to that user, without enormous waste. Humans work slowly compared with computers. Consequently, the computer would be idle most of the time while waiting for its user to initiate some action.

Timesharing was designed to make that kind of direct use efficient by enabling a computer to serve many users simultaneously. With such a system, each user sits at a terminal. The computer transfers its attention rapidly from one user to another, performing work as needed. Information is processed so quickly that the computer, in effect, appears to be totally dedicated to the work of each user.

Once the concept of timesharing had been incorporated, it became apparent that users did not have to be in the same room as the machine, but could communicate with it over communication lines from across the country or from anyplace in the world.

Thus, although large centralized systems continued to grow for applications such as recordkeeping and laborious computations for scientific research, the groundwork was laid in the 1960's for new types of computer use and new ways of designing systems to meet specific goals.

Computer trends in the 1970's: Communication-based computer systems and networks.

In the 1970's, communication-based computer systems began to grow. Some types of recordkeeping applications were obviously handled best by large central computers, but to be useful they needed immediate data entry and retrieval of information from remote locations.

Airline reservation systems, for example, were among the first large communication-based computer systems to be developed in the commercial sector. Reserving airline seats is clearly a complicated task, well-suited to computerization. Agents all over the country can now check flight availability and reserve seats from their work stations, both in "real time." (This term is used by technologists to refer to applications in which immediate action and response is provided by the computer.)

Another example of a large communication-based centralized computer system with decentralized access is the one operated by the National Association of Securities Dealers (NASD), known as NASDAQ (NASD Automatic Quotation.) It allows securities dealers instant access from their desks to the latest bid and ask prices for any stock listed on the over-the-counter market. The need here was clear for real time access to a data base by dealers across the country.

Another trend in the 1970's was the linking together of multiple computer systems—both small and large ones—into "networks." ARPANET, a project of the Department of Defense's Advanced Research Projects Agency (ARPA), was an ambitious and technically sophisticated experiment that linked together several large ARPA research computers over high-speed communication lines. This project was based on a new technique, called "packet switching," that allowed existing communication lines to be shared more efficiently for carrying computer data.

Future Trends in Computer-Based Information Systems

Three dominant economic factors can limit the range of computer applications:

1. the overall cost of computer hardware and the associated economies of scale;
2. the cost and difficulty of setting up and maintaining high-speed data communication links; and
3. the cost of producing software—the programs required to operate the system.

The first two limitations are being overcome. While there is still a strong market for large expensive systems, the cost of computing hardware has dropped to the point where, for many applications, possible economies of scale are offset by the overhead costs and the inconvenience of a large system. This trend is leading to the reliance on multiple smaller systems that are distributed geographically.

Several companies, American Telephone & Telegraph and Satellite Business Systems, for example, are building commercial data communication networks that promise to be economic, efficient, and convenient to use for linking together data systems and users.

The remaining problem, the cost of the software, is the pacesetting factor.[1] Progress has been slow in the development of new cost-cutting techniques for programing applications. For many applications serving a sizable user market, programing costs can be written off over a much larger user base. However, for a number of large specialized applications, the programing, maintenance, and operation costs will continue to be the dominant factors in the cost of using computers. Some experts see the software problem as the major obstacle to new applications of computers. For at least the first half of the 1980's, the cost of competent, sophisticated programing efforts will limit progress.

Based on the findings of this study, the use of computers will likely follow these trends in the 1980's.

- *Growth in the use of personal computers.* The small computer will become common both in the home and in business. Despite their small size, these systems will be highly capable—the equivalent of machines that sold for as much as $1 million in the 1950's. They may appear in the guise of video games, television sets, or telephones that will also have a computer capability available for other purposes. This trend will stimulate more widespread computer literacy in society, and in turn be reinforced by the consequent increase in the number of people able to program and use computers. The first generation to grow up with computers is now reaching maturity. These "computer literate" young adults accept computers as a natural part of their world. Computer design and use will be taught increasingly in school and as part of adult education, and will enhance an already thriving market for specialized application programs designed for small computers.
- *Expansion in the number and size of computer networks.* By the end of the decade, most computers, even small ones, will be connected to a communication network at least part of the time.

  The communication system may be dedicated to a single application in which all the machines on the network perform portions of a larger task. Public data networks, on the other hand, provide any home or business computer with access to a wide range of data bases or special programs that may be wanted for occasional use. Such multiuser national networks that can be interconnected now exist, and the number of users is expected to grow at a rapid rate.
- *The trend toward information services.* The computer industry has traditionally been concerned with selling hardware (desktop, mini, and mainframe computers and related auxiliary equipment). However, current trends in both pricing and the structure of the market are driving the emphasis toward providing computer-based information services, such as bibliographic and data base searches, electronic publishing, electronic banking, and the like. A number of these services will still require that the user possess a computer. However, many will be offered over data communication lines to homes and offices, and will be accessible through a modified ("intelligent") telephone or television set. Examples include two-way cable television, videotext, and the AT&T Electronic Information Services experiment that provides an electronic telephone directory over a telephone line to a home terminal. Eventually, information services of all kinds will dominate the data processing market in terms of dollar volume. (See ch. 14 for a detailed discussion.)
- *The competition among giant corporations for the data communication services market.* IBM, AT&T, Exxon, and GTE, among others, are preparing to offer a variety of data communication services.

[1] "Missing Computer Software," *Business Week*, Sept. 1, 1980, pp. 46-53.

Large corporations such as these have access to the capital required to install the technological base for the planned services, such as communication satellite systems and fiber optic transmission lines. A series of recent rulings by FCC, some still under challenge, are intended to clear the way for open competition among these and other corporations to provide information services of all kinds over communication lines. Resolution of the pending challenges by the courts or by Congress will have significant implications over the long term for the data communication industry. (See the OTA telecommunication study for a detailed discussion.[2])

At the same time, an examination of the computer industry (see ch. 14) shows that small entrepreneurs have frequently been innovators. This observation in no way discredits the valuable fundamental advances and product innovations originating from the research laboratories of large firms such as AT&T and IBM. However, creative new systems and innovative services increasingly arise from small, new, "spin-off" enterprises or from totally new entrants into the market.

Thus, faced with the dominance of the data communication field by large corporations, others in the information industry will press for a public policy that will guarantee access to data communication networks by smaller firms and new entrants that offer information services.

- *Higher level integration of data services.* Many individual networks for servicing specific corporate and governmental needs will continue to be built. Some of these networks will become integrated. For example, most airlines, car rental agencies, and large hotel chains have their own reservation systems. It is now technically feasible to build an integrated system that would provide travel agents access to all of these reservation systems through one desktop terminal.

  Similar integrated information systems are also feasible in insurance, banking, travel, entertainment, law enforcement, commodities exchanges, medical services, and many other sectors that now use several separate information systems. There are a number of factors such as system incompatibility, antitrust considerations, or competitive problems that may tend to resist this integration in the case of some systems.

- *The software bottleneck.* According to many computer and industry experts, the increasing capability of computer hardware is not being fully utilized due to problems encountered in creating suitable software programs for these new machines.[3] The major problems are the relatively slow increase in the productivity of programers—their cost efficiency—compared with that of the hardware, and the difficulties encountered in managing large programing projects.

  These problems have created bottlenecks in the development of new applications. Computer programing has been relatively resistant to productivity improvement, at least when compared with corresponding improvements in hardware performance. Programing is by nature labor intensive. Its cost is rising due to the increased programing requirements of new hardware coupled with a shortage of programing personnel with the needed training and experience. New mechanisms such as structured programing will be helpful in engineering computer programs and for managing their design and implementation.[4]

  At the other end of the scale, microtechnology is making possible enormous in-

[2]U.S. Congress, Office of Technology Assessment, *Telecommunication Technology and Public Policy Issues,* in press.

[3]Computer and Business Equipment Manufacturers Association, *Industry Forecast Panel: Productivity,* 1980 spring meeting.

[4]Some progress in improving software has been made by use of structured programing methods such as FORTH. See John S. James, "What is FORTH? A Tutorial Introduction," *Byte* magazine, August 1980, pp. 100ff.

creases in computational power through the creation of new hardware structures from clusters of small computer chips. Technologists know how to physically construct such combinations, but not how to use them as effectively as their potential would suggest.

Eliminating software bottlenecks may be the key to maintaining the lead in computer technology in the coming decade. In Japan, for example, the software problem has now been given a very high priority for R&D. In the United States, although a few defense agencies are investing in research to solve some of the problems, Federal R&D budgets for computer science and technology have not accorded software a similar priority. Private industry is the source of most activity in this area. Reportedly, one-third of the research effort at Bell Labs is devoted to the software problem.

Chapter 4
Information in Society

Contents

Chapter 4
Information in Society

The Information Society

An information industry analyst recently observed that "every society is an information society."[1] That is, all human organizations, no matter how simple, depend for their functioning on an intangible resource called "information." In any society, information serves several purposes. It can be, for example, a commodity of commerce, an indicator of wealth or power, a basis for making decisions, or a source of entertainment.

The more complex a society, the more central information is to its economic activities. The United States seems to be entering what some sociologists refer to as a "postindustrial" period,[2] characterized by several trends:

- emphasis is on a service economy rather than on manufacturing;
- information is used as a resource, as a factor of production, and as a commodity; and
- scientific discovery and technical innovation drive economic growth.

Whether or not this is a valid model of societal evolution, the above trends are no doubt taking place in the United States. Furthermore, they are combining to create a greater dependence on information processing and technology.

The tasks being undertaken by the large organizations that serve society are growing in complexity. The air traffic control system handles nearly 20 million flights yearly. Every year the financial system clears more than 30 billion checks, the U.S. Postal Service delivers over 100 billion pieces of mail, and the Internal Revenue Service (IRS) receives more than 140 million tax returns.

The service sector of the economy is growing at a relatively faster rate than the industrial and agricultural sectors (see fig. 6 in ch. 1). Many services such as medicine, law, education, and Government involve the transfer of large amounts of information. Resistance to productivity improvements in this sector, which represents a large part of the economy, has impeded overall productivity growth. Greater application of information technology has been proposed as a chief remedy. For this reason, it is highly likely that in this decade the service sector will increasingly depend on the use of computer-based information systems.

Greater international economic competition coupled with the decreasing availability of basic resources are requiring industry and Government to both improve and speed up their decisionmaking capabilities. Information technology is growing in importance for this purpose. Decisions about design, marketing, financing, and resource allocation all require a more sophisticated approach to the collection and use of information.

Computer and communication technologies, while not the direct causes of societal changes, are facilitating and in some cases accelerating them, thus helping generate the public policy issues confronting Congress. Some scholars see profound effects occurring from the increased dependence on computer technology, and predict that the view of humans as unique thinking beings will change fundamentally.[3] Others see significant shifts in the balance of power between individuals and the organizations, private

[1]Anthony G. Oettinger, "Information Resources: Knowledge and Power in the 21st Century," *Science Magazine*, vol. 209, July 1980, p. 191.

[2]Daniel Bell, *The Coming of the Post Industrial Society: A Venture in Social Forecasting* (New York: Basic Books, 1973).

[3]Bruce Mazlich, "The Fourth Discontinuity," *Technology and Culture 8*, pp. 1-15.

and governmental, that would directly affect our lives.[4] These highly speculative views raise important questions about the effects an extremely automated society might have on individual freedom. These questions need continued examination.

Some information policy experts take a more pragmatic view, one more useful for assessing specific public policy issues arising from the applications of this technology. Their approach stresses these two points:

1. It is not information technology per se that creates public policy issues, but the particular choices that are made concerning its use.
2. Most policy problems involving automated data systems are rooted in traditional institutional attitudes and procedures. Information systems must be assessed in the context of that history.

According to this view, technology itself does not restrict society to particular actions, but rather provides a widened range of choices.[5] Thus, it is not the impacts of a technology that are examined, but the impacts of the particular choices made. The nature of those choices is dependent on the social and legal environment in which they take place. For example, a totalitarian society would build information systems overtly designed to enhance Government control of its citizens. Such systems would be unacceptable in a democratic society.

The necessity of considering the historical context both of the systems and of the policy issues they raise is illustrated by the three case studies in the overall assessment.

1. The National Crime Information Center of the Federal Bureau of Investigation is an automated criminal record system that has been in existence for only 13 years. Yet the patterns of its use, the types of data stored, and the profound public policy issues it raises are the same as those prevalent over the past 100 years of recordkeeping in the criminal justice community.
2. The Postal Service is nearly as old as this Nation, and the telegraph is almost 150 years old. The distinction between physical and electrical transmission of messages that has existed for a long time without creating serious problems is now being challenged. However, over the years the Postal Service has become an integral part of American society. Decisions about its future role with respect to electronic mail need to take into account all of its historical roles: as a service provider, as an employer, and as an agent for social communication and connection on which many sectors of U.S. society depend.
3. Banking has existed since ancient times. Electronic funds transfer systems are not so much changing the nature of banking as they are helping alter traditional institutional practices in the United States, such as restrictions on multistate banking, distinctions between types of banking institutions, and limitations on types of financial services. The issues of privacy and security, which are examined in some detail in chapters 6 and 7, historically have seriously concerned the banking community, and are thus shaped by its traditional attitudes and practices.

The Nature of Information

The role of information in society is being changed under the influence of new information technology. Some of the changes taking place are:

- Information is becoming a significant economic commodity, but one with certain unique characteristics that distinguish it from conventional commodities of commerce.
- The industry providing information technology and information services

[4]A. Mowshowitz, *The Conquest of Will* (Reading, Mass.: Addison-Wesley, 1976).

[5]Daniel Bell, "Communications Technology—For Better or For Worse," *Harvard Business Review*, May-June 1979, p. 20.

has become a major component of the U.S. economy.

- Many more individuals, both as workers and as citizens, need more information and information technology to function effectively.

Thus, over the next two decades information technology will likely change production processes and commercial goods, transportation and working patterns, the nature and content of education, the content and style of entertainment, and the way social values are formed and political decisions made.

There are three basic values of information: commercial, private, and public (see fig. 7 in ch. 1). Information technology is changing the relative importance of these values and throwing them into conflict.[6]

The Commercial Value of Information

Information has been a commodity of commerce for centuries. Books and newspapers, and in this century the broadcasting industry, all sell information. The classic reference book on knowledge as a commodity was written in 1962.[7] The value of information increases as society becomes more dependent on it. The very high growth rate of the computer-based information industry illustrates this trend (see ch. 14).

Information, particularly in a technological environment, has characteristics that distinguish it from more tangible commodities.

- It is reproducible. Its theft does not deny it to the original owner.
- The cost of its reproduction is usually very low compared with that of its original assembly or creation.
- It can be transported instantly anywhere in the Nation or the world over communication lines.
- Its lifetime, which can be very brief, is thus a principal determinant of its value.
- Its value is not additive. Two or more copies of the same item of information are not necessarily worth much more to the possessor than one.

These characteristics, magnified in some cases by the technology, have created policy problems with respect to computer crime, copyright and patent laws, the flow of data between nations, and property tax laws. The traditional rules and procedures of the U.S. economic and legal systems are oriented toward the commercial exchange of tangible goods and services rather than of information.

The Private Value of Information

In an information society, economic competition is often based on access to special information, such as a formula for a soft drink, an econometric projection, marketing plans, or geological data. Commercially important information is considered by organizations to be proprietary.

Similarly, individuals often consider information about themselves to be private, either because damage can be done by its disclosure or simply because they desire to be left alone. (See ch. 7 on privacy for a more complete discussion.)

The Public Value of Information

American society has always viewed information as having a public value, and has asserted the public interest in a free flow of information. There are many examples:

- the public support of libraries, schools, and museums to produce an informed and literate citizenry;

[6]For a related discussion see Louis H. Mayo, Robert W. Anthony, Henry B. Freedman, et al., *An Exploratory Assessment of Computer-Assisted Makeup and Imaging Systems* (Washington, D.C.: The George Washington University Program of Policy Studies in Science and Technology, January 1980).

[7]F. Machlup, *The Production and Distribution of Knowledge in the United States* (Princeton, N.J.: Princeton University Press, 1962).

- a tradition of academic freedom and a system of open scholarly publication to promote the exchange of ideas and the advance of research;
- first amendment guarantees, which ensure an unfettered discussion of political ideas, freedom of religion, and a free press; and
- freedom of information laws asserting the rights of citizens to know as much as possible about the actions of their Government.

These examples suggest that there is an assumption that American society has a right of access to information of various kinds, and that it is in the public interest to facilitate that access.

This principle has historically brought Government into opposition with private sector interests. Public education competes with private, libraries compete with booksellers, and so on. In the past, these conflicts have not been serious. As the information society grows, however, and the economic value of information rises, conflicts over its access and use will increase in severity and become more difficult to resolve. Additional problems will be caused by changes in the technologies for the distribution of information, such as the replacement of certain books by aggregations of articles delivered electronically.

The social interest in guaranteeing equitable access to information may conflict with the need to encourage private sector investment in new information services by letting a profitable market develop. It can also be argued that improvements in the quality of information available to decisionmakers both in the public and private sectors would reduce errors in the allocation of resources, thereby benefiting society as a whole.

Many Federal agencies—the Census Bureau, IRS, the Securities and Exchange Commission, the Environmental Protection Agency, and the Federal Elections Commission, to name just a few—collect large and, in most cases, growing amounts of information, which could be personal or proprietary. The right of the Government to collect the information is established in law, presumably to further legitimate public purposes. However, such collection may strongly conflict with what individuals and organizations believe to be their rights of privacy, and thereby creates an obligation on the Government to protect the information and use it only in carefully prescribed ways.

The Information Economy

Information plays a significant economic role in U.S. society. The number of companies that manufacture and supply computer and communication services is very large and still growing more rapidly than the overall gross national product. The U.S. computer industry, which sold over $40 billion worth of hardware in 1979, has a projected annual growth rate for the near future of around 20 percent; and the worldwide communication industry, which in 1979 had revenues of over $60 billion, has a projected annual growth rate of about 8½ percent.

Another measure of the economic importance of these industries is that AT&T and IBM are two of the largest corporations in the world. AT&T ranks first and IBM is among the top five American industrial corporations. (The computer industry is examined in more detail in ch. 14.)

Information services, a new but increasingly important industrial sector, use computer and communication technologies to provide new types of products and services. Some of these are:

- Teletext service, which provides certain types of consumer information (e.g., airline schedules, news reports, shopping guides) over a regular television broadcast signal. This transmission of information does not interfere with the regular video program and can be accessed with a special decoder on a standard television receiver.
- Computerizd paging services, which provide elaborate remote messaging services by means of microcomputers in the paging unit itself.
- Specialized information services, which are built into the voice telephone network.

This very young, small, innovative, and rapidly growing industry will be the exploiter of the potentially large consumer markets for information technology services. (Information services are further examined briefly in ch. 14.)

In addition to the above-mentioned sectors of the information economy, there is a much broader sector. It was first studied and characterized in 1976.[8] In this analysis, the two sectors of the information economy were identified as primary and secondary.

The primary information sector includes those who generate and sell information as well as those who produce information technology, and is much more comprehensive than the computer and communication sectors. Included are typewriter manufacturers, newspaper publishers, producers of films, and broadway and television shows.

The secondary information sector is comprised of information services and products used by any organization for its own internal purposes. Examples are internal accounting and production, management, and inventory control systems, many of which are already computerized.

An examination of the trends in the work force reveals the extent to which the economy has shifted. The results of the 1976 analysis shown graphically in figure 6 (see ch. 1) illustrate the transitions from an economy dominated by agriculture, to one dominated by manufacturing, to a service and information economy. It can also be seen that the growth of the information sector did not start with the invention of the computer, but considerably earlier.

Because macroeconomic studies such as these are so broad, they tend to blur the line between industries that use information systems and those few remaining activities that are presently not directly affected by this technology. However, the line separating these two sectors is shifting rapidly and social impacts can flow across it. Thus, for example:

- computer graphics are changing the operating style of the film animation industry;
- traditional print publishers such as Readers Digest and the Knight-Ridder newspapers have invested in new inhouse computer/communication-based information services to reach the public;
- the nature of public education may be transformed by new competing information delivery systems; and
- computer-based systems for delivering television programing tailored to each home will change the role of network broadcasting in the United States.

The transformation of much of the information industry that is being brought about by new information systems will change the structure of the industry, the nature of the services provided, and the skills needed by its employees.

As technology reduces the cost as well as the experience and training required for information retrieval, public library services, even in small cities and towns, will increasingly supply more and more up-to-date information from a variety of sources. In many countries, automated card catalogs on ma-

---

[8]Marc Porat, *The Information Economy,* Ph. D. dissertation, Institute for Communication Research, Stanford University, Stanford, California, 1976.

nipulatable filmstrips, and newspapers and periodicals on microfilm and microfiche, are expanding the resources of libraries in schools, universities, and industry. However, this trend may conflict with the public value of information, to the extent libraries move in the direction of charging fees for access to electronic information services. This would run counter to the current free access policies of most public libraries.

Entire editions of newspapers and newsletters are centrally written and electronically duplicated and transmitted—via satellite and microwave—to regional plants where they are printed and disseminated. High-quality transmission of photographs and schematic drawings can accompany the texts of these publications in a matter of minutes after the text is sent.

The emerging and expanding information technologies are reducing the costs and improving the accessibility of many kinds of information. Their impact is also being felt in the traditional hard print industries, which must adapt their conventional ways of doing business to the new technologies or risk displacement by more technologically sophisticated competitors entering the marketplace.

Some economists are beginning to examine the information economy. They are building information into traditional economic theory and modifying economic models to incorporate information as a commodity or factor of production. Although this work is still in its early stages, it will be important in the development of usable economic models for the next quarter of a century.

Chapter 5
The Structure of Information Policy

Contents

LIST OF TABLES

Chapter 5
The Structure of Information Policy

Introduction to Information Law and Regulation

Current policies governing information systems are a composite of many specific regulations and laws, which are based on three main factors:

1. The areas affected or the regulatory concerns (privacy, freedom of information, etc.).
2. The affected sector of society (banking, education, Government, etc.).
3. The lawmakers and/or rulemakers (Congress, the Federal Communications Commission, State legislatures, etc.)

In the course of this study, OTA identified 14 areas of law and regulation that affect information systems or are affected by them. The classification shown in table 4 illustrates the breadth of legal and regulatory involvement and the range of participants, but does not reflect the variety of information systems users (e.g., banking, insurance, Government, or education). The applicable laws and regulations vary according to the particular sector involved.

Such a diversity of concerns cannot be encompassed by any single simple policy formulation. Computer users face a confusing array of laws and regulations unless consideration is given to their overall pattern—their overlaps, their contradictions, and their deficiencies. Continuation of the present situation could inhibit many socially desirable applications of information systems or could create even more intractable policy problems in the future.

The term "information policy" as it has been used to describe the Federal Government's involvement in this area is somewhat misleading. First, it is too broadly applied in reference to a miscellany of issues that include, for example, the regulation of files of personal data, Federal support of the Nation's libraries, first amendment rights for newspapers, and property rights associated with information products such as programs and data bases.

Second, the term appears to suggest that there is or should be a single uniform policy governing all the uses of information systems both in the public and private sectors.

Table 4.—Principal Areas of Law and Regulation Regarding Information Systems

Area of concern	State	Federal	Regulatory	Court[a]	International
Privacy	X	X		X	X
Freedom of information	X	X		X	X
First amendment		X	X	X	
Fourth amendment		X		X	
Due process	X	X	X	X	
Communications regulations	X	X	X	X	X
Computer crime	X	X		X	
Proprietary rights		X		X	
Evidence	X	X	X	X	
Liability	X	X		X	
Antitrust		X	X	X	
Taxation	X	X			X
Government provision of information	X	X			X
Government procurement of information systems	X	X			

[a]Involvement that creates new law or interpretation.

SOURCE: OTA working paper on "The Legal/Regulatory Environment of Information Systems," June 1980.

In fact, no such policy exists, nor does one appear to be likely.

The analysis made by OTA has led to these findings:

- There appears to be neither a strong trend nor sentiment at present among policymakers in favor of a uniform Federal information policy that would encompass all the problems that could arise from the many possible uses of data systems.*

*Some recently proposed legislation would establish a comprehensive approach to certain specific problem areas, e.g., privacy and freedom of information. See H.R. 2465, 96th Cong., "Omnibus Right to Privacy Act of 1979." Also, the National Telecommunications and Information Administration (NTIA) of the Department of Commerce has made an effort to formulate—or at least develop a framework for—national information policies. See Arthur A. Bushkin and Jane H. Yurow, *The Foundations of United States Information Policy,* (Washington, D.C., NTIA, June 1980) and Jane H. Yurow, et al., *Issues in Information Policy,* Helen A. Shaw (ed.), NTIA, February, 1981.

- There are numerous laws and regulations, some overlapping and some potentially or actually conflicting, that directly and indirectly affect the users of information systems, the consumers of information services, and the subjects of personal information data banks.
- There is a lack of congressional focus on information policy as such, and consequently the emerging issues are not being directly addressed.*

*The "Paperwork Reduction Act of 1980" (Public Law 96-511) enacted by the 96th Congress does set out a more comprehensive policy and management approach for Federal Government information systems. The Act establishes within the Office of Management and Budget an Office of Information and Regulatory Affairs and assigns to that Office a broad range of authorities and required actions.

Structure of Policy Issues

Few attempts have been made at integrating the whole range of policy issues covered by the term "information." The subject area relating to computers and public policy, however, is being increasingly analyzed. A wide range of intellectual approaches are being taken, from narrow quantitative studies of the impacts of information systems on corporate decisionmaking and the problems associated with implementation,[1] to broad philosophical and historical examinations of the long-term social effects of automating information systems.[2] [3] [4]

[1]Henry Lucas, *Why Information Systems Fail* (New York: Columbia University Press, 1975).

[2]James Rule, *Private Lives and Public Surveillance: Social Control in the Computer Age* (New York: Schocken Books, 1974).

[3]K. Laudon, *Computers and Bureaucratic Reform* (New York: Wiley-Interscience, 1974).

[4]Abby Mowshowitz, *The Conquest of Will: Information Processing in Human Affairs* (Reading, Mass.: Addison-Wesley, 1976).

Several studies have been carried out and commissions formed to examine various aspects and issues related to information policy. In the field of privacy alone, for example, there have been a study project by the National Academy of Sciences,[5] an advisory committee to the Secretary of Health, Education, and Welfare, a Privacy Protection Study Commission, and a number of studies and hearings conducted by congressional committees. Of the more than 1,500 legislative proposals submitted to either the House or the Senate during the 95th Congress, 74 new public laws emerged dealing with some aspect of information law or policy. Of these, 26 dealt with privacy, disclosure of information, confidentiality or controls on data, and transactions using computers.[6]

[5]Alan Westin and Michael A. Baker, *Databanks in a Free Society* (New York: Quadrangle Books, 1972).

[6]U.S. House of Representatives, Committee on House Administration, *Information Policy: Public Laws From the 95th Congress,* Jan. 31, 1979.

Another indication of the extent of activity is the *Congressional Research Service Listing of New and Completed Projects.* It covers ongoing work and projects completed within the last 6 months that have been carried out by the Congressional Research Service, the General Accounting Office, the Office of Technology Assessment, and the Congressional Budget Office. The most recent listing available to this study, published on August 25, 1980, described nearly 100 projects concerned with computer and telecommunication policy. The issues addressed by all of these activities can be classified under one or more of the categories shown in table 5.

System Issues

The policy issues related to information systems per se focus on their design, implementation, and operation. They generally are concerned with whether the system performs the tasks expected of it with reliability, with appropriate security, and in an efficient and timely manner. These objectives mainly are of interest to the organization operating the system, and place major constraints on the system designer.

Other system issues include the proper role of users in system design, the need for user education, and how to deal with potential system impacts on the organizations, work groups, and individuals involved. While skilled technically, system designers may not fully appreciate the implications for users. On the other hand, users frequently do not understand enough about the system itself.

Technical, operational, and reliability factors all can have broader societal significance even though they originate in the operational goals of the system itself. In recent years, for example, public attention has been focused on areas such as:

- the safety and reliability of the air traffic control system;
- the reliability, security, and controllability of military command and control systems, existing and proposed;
- the security of large-scale electronic funds transfer systems; and
- the reliability, accuracy, and responsiveness of the social security information systems.

There is a strong societal interest in the proper and reliable technical operation of

Table 5.—Structure of Information Policy Issues

Level of issues	Character of issues	Example issues
System level	Relate to the design, implementation, and operation of particular information systems	Government procurement policy. Efficiency and economy of operation. Security of information systems.
Information level	Relate to the handling of data: collection, storage, use, and dissemination	Privacy (recordkeeping). Freedom of Information regulations. Copyright and patents as related to computer programs.
Secondary policy impacts	Exist independent of the particular information systems, but are changed in magnitude or character by use of technology.	Privacy (surveillance). First amendment rights. Fourth amendment rights. Social vulnerability. Federal-State relations.
Long-term societal effects	Long-range societal impacts that are not currently reflected in specific policy problems, but which may ultimately affect the nature of U.S. society.	Privacy (social attitudes). Psychological self-image of humans. Education needs. Social-political effects. Cultural impacts.

SOURCE: Office of Technology Assessment.

each of the systems cited above, and potentially high costs to society if they fail. The public policy issues that arise are those associated with the formulation of a framework within which to develop the systems, to establish accountability for their design and operation, to assign responsibility for correcting their defects, and to mitigate the impacts of system failures.

Information Issues

Various laws and regulations affect the use of information, independent of the particular technology employed in handling it. As we become more and more an "information society," these legalities have a correspondingly greater impact on the activities of individuals and organizations. Since the laws and regulations arise from many sources and thus do not reflect a single coherent view of the role of information in society, they tend to conflict and to have unintended effects on the operation of information systems. Consequently, they can create unanticipated secondary effects.

The three differing fundamental values of information—commercial, private, and public—discussed in chapter 4 motivate the laws and regulations affecting information. Individual regulations or laws usually address only one aspect of information. Policy issues, then, arise from the inherent tensions between the particular values reflected in different laws. Congress is called on to establish equitable balances. For example:

- Freedom of information laws (reflecting public value) can conflict with individual or proprietary concerns (reflecting private values). For example, in serving the public interest, Government collects an extraordinary amount of information about citizens, businesses, and other types of organizations. Some of this information that theoretically has been available to the public by law for a long time has been protected, in fact, by the amount of effort required to retrieve it from manual recordkeeping systems. Automated systems reduce the cost and time barriers to wider access to these public records, and thereby may accentuate the issue of the extent to which this information can and should be publicly available.
- As information becomes a more valuable commercial commodity, increasing tensions are arising between those who wish to sell it through new information services, and those who recommend that the Government take steps to prevent the social inequity that would possibly result from the increasing cost of access to information and the means to use it. For example, the conflict is likely to become heightened between the evolving role of the public libraries as seen by the librarians, and the new companies that wish to sell similar information services to the home. Related tensions stem from the competition between Government-collected data, made available through freedom of information laws, and commercial data services. In addition, commercially marketable information may invade privacy or proprietary rights.
- The controversy over the public v. the commercial value of information is exemplified by the present difficulty that the United States is having in formulating a consistent national position with respect to international negotiations concerning information transmission across borders. Laws have already been promulgated by several European nations restricting the flow of personal or corporate data across their borders.

Some positions taken by the United States appear to advocate the free flow of information on the premise that information is a public good, and therefore should be allowed to flow freely between countries. The United States appears to emphasize the commodity-related aspects of information, maintaining that controls or restrictions are, in effect, restraint of trade. While this position would presumably allow U.S.

multinational firms to more freely deliver and sell information services across borders, it may have adverse implications for the international protection of individual privacy.

Secondary Policy Impacts

Computer-based information systems, by increasing the quantity of information collected, the efficiency of its collection and dissemination, its utility, and its ease of storage can cause qualitative changes in the behavior of Government, individuals, and organizations as well as in the nature of traditional conflicts. Thus, the use of automated information systems can have secondary effects on policy problems that have existed for years, and which in many ways are independent of the technology. Because much more information can be obtained, handled, processed, and distributed so much faster, old problems are not merely exacerbated, but new ones are created.

For example, the increased scale and presumed efficiency of automated criminal justice recordkeeping intensifies the tension society has always experienced between the needs of law enforcement and the individual rights of citizens. Similarly, the tendency of the technology to encourage centralized record systems creates problems of Federal/State relationships, a particularly touchy issue in law enforcement. Some experts believe this centralization trend could reverse through the use of smaller computers with distributed data bases. The OTA study of the National Crime Information Center Computerized Criminal History system, being conducted in parallel with this study, examines this set of issues and relationships in detail.

Electronic mail will once more raise issues of the inviolability of the mail. The rules governing access are different for letters and for telegrams. Which will take precedence in the new environment? Will the first amendment rights enjoyed by the printed news media or the tradition of the Federal Communications Commission's regulation of content be the pattern for protecting the new electronic information media?

Ongoing issues such as privacy, security, and social equity are still not resolved. Electronic funds transfer (EFT), by changing the scale and nature of information collection and storage in an environment of accelerating institutional changes in the industry, may be forcing the reconsideration of such issues in a totally new technological context. The OTA study of EFT, being conducted in parallel, examines these issues in greater detail.

Computers may not only cause policy problems but may also be useful in solving them, and information systems may have policy impacts that mitigate or enhance the resolution of other policy conflicts. For example, it has been suggested that a central computer file containing information about citizens and employable aliens would be useful in verifying employability while avoiding the complicated problems created by a national I.D. card. (This suggestion is not intended to be an endorsement of such a system.) Transmitting electronic mail in a coded form (encryption) could help resolve social concerns over wiretapping or mail tampering. Services available through EFT, such as check authorization/guarantee and debit cards, can facilitate payment by other means than cash and thereby provide an additional convenience to customers.

Long-Term Societal Effects

Social scientists engaged in futures studies have suggested that the information revolution, spurred both by advances in computers and communication and by the changing role of information in U.S. society, will have profound long-term effects as dramatic as those caused by the invention of the printing press.

While such effects may, in fact, be socially significant in the long term, they are also the most difficult to predict and to relate directly to particular public policy choices. For example:

- The nature of societal values attached to privacy in the United States may change if larger and more ubiquitous information systems gradually remove the ability of individuals to hide their private activities. The permanency of data storage and ease of recall can limit a criminal's ability to start over with a clean slate. It has been pointed out that the possession by large organizations of personal data on individuals enhances the power, real or perceived, of the organization over the person.[7] [8] These and similar effects may increase the suspicion some citizens have of large organizations—business, labor, or Government—and thus erode social cooperation and a personal sense of well-being.
- The self-image held by humans of their uniqueness, distinguished by their ability to think, may be threatened by the association with machines that increasingly demonstrate apparent characteristics of intelligence.[9] Computer scientists disagree about whether truly "intelligent" systems can ever be built. In the creation of social attitudes, however, the perception of machine omnipotence may be as important as reality. The best chess machines already can beat 99.5 percent of human players.

  One effect of such a perception may be to increase the uncritical reliance on computers.[10] The general public's unquestioning acceptance of computer output has concerned computer experts for many years, and may be a contributing factor in criminal acts that use computer-generated information to establish credibility.
- Just as the printing press, by stimulating literacy and speeding the flow of ideas, supported the Renaissance and the transition from medieval society to the age of enlightenment, so the new information systems could profoundly transform the social and political environment of U.S. and world society. Indeed television and sophisticated computer-based polling technology have already had observable effects on the political processes in the United States. Third World leaders calling in UNESCO for a "new world information order" express the belief that information technology will have a central influence on the social and economic development of their countries as well as on international relationships.
- The effects of information technology on culture have received little study. Years ago, the noted Canadian economic historian Harold Adams Innes (and later his student, Marshall McLuhan) discussed the profound effects on cultural biases exerted by the forms in which information is communicated.[11] [12]

  Scholarly opinions differ concerning the nature of these effects. Some see in broadcast television a lowering of social values and a reduction in literacy, a debasing of culture resulting from mass communication. However, a single television broadcast of a Metropolitan Opera performance reaches more viewers than have attended the Met in all its years of existence. Has "Sesame Street" improved the educational level of its viewers, or has it conditioned young children to a short attention span and to an orientation toward learning as entertainment, unsuitable for serious academic work?

This overview study has not attempted to address in detail these broader questions. The conflicts and problems are only identified here. Given the potential for significant social change, good or bad, research funded publicly, privately, or in some jointly

[7]Laudon, op. cit.

[8]Westin and Baker, op. cit.

[9]S. Turkle, "Computer as Rorschach," *Society*, vol. 17, No. 2, January/February 1980, pp. 15-24.

[10]J. Weizenbaum, *Computer Power and Human Reason* (San Francisco: W. H. Freeman & Co., 1976).

[11]House of Representatives, op. cit.

[12]Turkle, op. cit.

developed projects could provide valuable insights into the long-term societal effects of computer-based information systems and related public policy choices.

The categories shown in table 5 are not independent of each other. Policies at various governmental and industrial levels interact with one another in areas such as the economy. In a similar way, there is a complex interaction between the categories. Procedures set for system operation may affect problems of information handling in response, for example, to privacy regulations. Rules for the handling of information may exacerbate or mitigate secondary policy impacts. On the other hand, they may also affect the way in which specific systems are designed and operated.

Various concerned parties view these issues from their particular perspectives. For example, an agency wishing to install a major new information system may be motivated by considerations of system utility: whether the system will do its intended job and be economical to run, and whether the procurement has been handled fairly. Congress, in addition to being interested in the system's effectiveness, also wants to know whether it satisfies a broader set of requirements, for example, whether it conforms to a number of information policy constraints such as protection of civil liberties, individual privacy, or freedom of information laws, and how the system might affect these as well as other less well-defined secondary policy issues.

Finally, as critics of information technologies and systems express concerns about the long-term social effects that may or may not occur, it has become apparent that these effects would be difficult, if not impossible, to address solely through a legislative approach. Congress can only seek to establish a legislative basis for creating a balance between the public/social values, the commercial/economic values, and the privacy/proprietary values associated with information. The stresses within that triad remain in a dynamic state. They are exacerbated or mitigated by many other social factors in addition to lawmaking and policy formulation. Society has not as yet learned how to predict the consequences of manipulating the numerous factors involved.

Chapter 6
Innovation, Productivity, and Employment

Contents

Chapter 6
Innovation, Productivity, and Employment

Introduction

Innovation, the continual generation of new technological ideas and products and services based on those ideas, is a prime requisite for a healthy industry in a high technology field. Congress and the executive branch have been particularly concerned about possible economic and regulatory incentives to innovation. The Congressional Research Service (CRS) identified 30 separate bills concerned with stimulating innovation that were considered by the 96th Congress.[1] A major executive branch study coordinated by the Secretary of Commerce culminated, in October 1979, in a Presidential message to Congress on industrial innovation, in which a number of measures were proposed.[2]

Information technology is central to these concerns. Computer and communication technologies are moving ahead so rapidly that products can become obsolete within a few years. Thus, although the United States holds a substantial positive balance of trade in certain areas of computer technology, the maintenance of this balance depends on continued research and development (R&D). Because of aggressive import competition from Europe, Japan, and Canada, even domestic markets are vulnerable to any faltering in the technological lead. A parallel OTA study is examining U.S. industrial competitiveness in the international electronics and computer markets.[3]

[1]Congressional Research Service, "Industrial Innovation," issue brief No. IB 80005; updated 10/24/80.

[2]U.S. Congress, House of Representatives, "Industrial Innovation message from the President of the United States transmitting proposals for Fostering Industrial Innovation," Oct. 31, 1979, Washington, D.C. (96th Cong., 1st sess., House, Doc. 96-214).

[3]U.S. Congress, Office of Technology Assessment, *Assessment of Impact of Technology on Competitiveness of U.S. Electronics Industry*, in progress.

Research and Development

The structure of innovation and product development in the computer industry is unusual, even for a high technology field. Basic research in computer science, which is largely carried out in universities, is based on the technology rather than on physical laws.[4] Thus, the leadtime between a fundamental theoretical advance in computer science and a practical application is, in general, relatively short, a few years or less.

Because of this close connection between technology and research, the vitality of the computer industry is in part dependent on the vitality of academic computer science. However, university departments of computer science are experiencing problems.[5] Rapidly growing departments face competition with private industry for the talented faculty needed to do the research and to train new experts. This situation is particularly critical in systems design and soft-

[4]Bruce Arden (ed.), *What Can Be Automated?* report of the Computer Science and Engineering Research Study (Cambridge, Mass.: Massachusetts Institute of Technology Press, 1980).

[5]National Science Foundation, *Science and Engineering Education for the 1980's and Beyond: A Report to the President*, October 1980.

ware engineering. The departments also need to invest in the facilities necessary for R&D and in experimental* computer science.

Several U.S. corporations in the information industry, realizing that their success depends on continued innovation, have established their own large research centers. Bell Laboratories in the United States and IBM both here and overseas are notable examples. These centers produce outstanding basic and applied research, and are also important links between the basic research carried out in the universities and the needs of industry.

*Experimental computer science tries to develop new concepts of computer architecture and programing by working directly with the machines rather than through theoretical analysis. Many vital areas of computer science cannot yet be addressed through theory. They are approached through the experience of developing programs to do particular tasks.

Another aspect of innovation in the information industry is the role played by small entrepreneurial firms in new product development. Many specialized areas at the leading edge of information technology are dominated by relatively small new companies (see ch. 14). Indeed, some experts in the industry suggest that one important pattern for innovation in information technology involves an entrepreneur who develops a new product and then forms a company to produce and sell it. If successful, the new company's need for capital expands. Frequently in the last decade, the only choice for the small company to meet this capital need was to be acquired by a larger firm. This is still the predominant goal of most high technology, high growth companies, although a few have been able to reach the public market.

Productivity

In the 1970's, the rate of productivity growth in the United States fell far below historical trends, causing concern in Government and industry. In addition to providing the basis for an increased standard of living, productivity growth is a major defense against inflationary pressures, especially those caused by cost increases for externally provided resources such as oil. (Electronics and agriculture, two sectors that have experienced very high productivity growth rates, have supplied the principal exports offsetting the large international trade imbalance due to oil imports.) Productivity growth also provides the leeway to meet certain societal goals, such as a more equitable distribution of basic goods and services like food, medical care, and education.

Although not all economists agree on the causes of the productivity lag, four main factors in the last decade have commonly been noted by various experts:

- growth of the service sector of the economy,
- entry into the job market of a large number of young and inexperienced workers,
- decline in the rate of technical innovation and investments in R&D, and
- growing Federal intervention in the form of regulation and tax policies that discourage innovation.

There is reason to believe that innovation in computer technology can help productivity growth in the United States. In addition to lower cost and/or better quality retail consumer products, the new technology also generates improved techniques and tools for making those products. Experts have noted the positive correlation between innovation rates and productivity in several industries.[6]

Based on anticipated advances in artificial intelligence, robotics, computer control, and input-output technology over the next few

[6]Edwin Mansfield, "Research and Development, Productivity, and Inflation," *Science*, vol. 209, Sept. 5, 1980, pp. 1,091-1,093.

years, computer-based factory automation will make a substantial contribution to improving manufacturing productivity. Word processing and other forms of office automation are already responsible for improving clerical productivity and may have similar potential for managerial productivity. Intelligent cash registers and automated checkout are directly improving the productivity of retail clerks and indirectly the productivity of retail management (e.g., accounting, inventory control, procurement). Automated bank tellers (teller machines) are reducing the service loads on human tellers. The full impact is yet to be felt of these and other applications that are only now starting to be installed in the service sector. However, they are likely to help restore an upward trend in the Nation's productivity.

From a larger societal perspective, the increased productivity brought about by advances in computer technology may be reflected not only in greater output per employee, but perhaps also in terms of better product quality, improved work environment and job satisfaction, and longer term social benefits such as improved job safety and greater opportunities for on-the-job learning and career advancement.

Unemployment

It is self-evident that any innovation that creates new products and new industries will eliminate some jobs only to create others. Structural shifts in the economy will occur to the distress of the temporarily displaced.

An innovation that creates a demand for highly skilled programers while eliminating the jobs of low-level clerical workers causes hardship through a short- to medium-term increase in unemployment. In certain industries, such as insurance, automation has caused a significant reduction in clerical staff.

Some believe that the nature of labor displacement should be examined in more detail since there are likely to be marked differences between the well-recorded experience of computing technology's first quarter of a century and the coming decades. Some of these differences are said to include:

- *Cheaper and readily available communication and computer technology,* which allows previously labor-intensive jobs—such as sales clerks, bank tellers, and secretaries—to be automated.
- *New research results* in fields such as process control, robotics, and the interface between humans and machines, which widen the applicability of computer automation. The "automated factory," a completely automated shop capable of manufacturing a wide variety of products on demand without human intervention, may become a reality in the next decade or two.

The assessment of the role of the U.S. Postal Service in electronic mail is the only study in OTA's examination of three national information systems to specifically look at employment impacts. Preliminary research results suggest that electronically transmitted mail would likely eliminate postal jobs as the volume of conventional mail decreases. However, it appears that the rate of such job displacement would be unlikely to exceed ordinary attrition. Further research is focusing on the rate of job displacement and possible geographical discrepancies, the need for job retraining, the impacts on levels and costs of service, and the broader implications for the future of the U.S. Postal Service.[7]

[7]U.S. Congress, Office of Technology Assessment, *Preliminary Assessment of the Role of the U.S. Postal Service in Electronic Message Services,* in progress.

Issues

Congress will be confronting a number of issues concerned with innovation in computer technology and its effects on productivity and employment.

R&D Support

For a number of years the vitality of U.S. science and technology has depended, in part, on Federal support. In times of low productivity gains, taxpayer resistance to increased governmental spending is understandable as pressure grows to trim programs, such as R&D, that do not satisfy immediate needs. There has been a similar tendency by some sectors in private industry to cut R&D budgets when money is tight. Industry also cites tax disincentives to R&D investment, particularly prior to the 1978 capital gains tax reduction.

Innovation in information technology improves the productivity of the information industry itself and also offers the tools for improving the productivity of many other sectors of the economy. Therefore, some believe Federal R&D support is a wise policy, particularly in light of international competition for the same markets.

Research in basic computer science is supported by the National Science Foundation (NSF), the Office of Naval Research, the Advanced Projects Research Agency, and to a lesser extent by a few other agencies. Applied R&D is supported by NSF and by mission agencies such as the National Aeronautics and Space Administration and the Department of Energy, although the major part of development support comes from the Department of Defense. One issue to consider is whether research in the applications of computer technology to problems in the private (civilian) sector—in such areas as education, health, transportation, environmental quality, and job safety—is receiving adequate Federal support, given the critical nature of computer technology to the Nation's well-being.

Computer Impact Research

The very applicability and power for change inherent in computer technology that makes it so promising as a means of solving many societal problems has raised concerns that it might also have negative effects. Many computer and social scientists, aware of these potential problems, have been developing a field of research on computer impacts.[8] Professional journals have been started, courses are being developed, and a few computer scientists are describing their principal professional interest to be "computer impacts." To date, however, it has been difficult to secure much Federal support for research because this subject does not comfortably fit into traditional scientific basic research programs, and because the products of early research tended to be of mixed quality.

Computer impact research is not pure computer science; neither is it classifiable as purely social or political science. It is also of no direct interest to the mission agencies, such as the Departments of Energy and Defense. However, the kinds of data and ideas that could be generated by long-term research in the societal impacts of computers could supply valuable input to the executive branch and to congressional agencies such as the General Accounting Office, CRS, and OTA. In addition, this research could help public officials and administrators gain a broader perspective of the social, economic, political, and institutional issues involved with managing information resources and technology in Government.[9]

---

[8]R. L. Kling, "Social Issues and Impacts of Computing: From Arena to Discipline," *Proceedings of the 2d Conference on Computers and Human Choice,* Vienna, Austria, June 1979.

[9]See Donald A. Marchand, "Are Public Administrators Failing To Do Their Computer Homework?" *Government Data Systems,* September/October 1980, p. 22 ff.

Employment

It is still uncertain whether the productivity increases brought about by computer technology will create or eliminate jobs. It would be helpful to know more about the long-term effects of automation. It is assumed that there will be some local structural impacts. Even if new jobs are created or old ones redefined, not all workers will find it easy or desirable to shift. This dislocation could result even when an official policy of no job loss has been established by a company, if employees are unwilling or unable to adapt themselves to the new technology or prove to be untrainable in the new procedures.

One OTA advisory panel member observed that, in periods of high demand and relatively full employment, labor displacement is unlikely to occur; however, when trying to pull out of a period of high unemployment there is greater incentive for firms to make productivity gains by investing in automation rather than increasing their labor force. Substituting machines for labor is easier when it can be done by not hiring when market demand for the product increases rather than having to fire.

On the other hand, it can be argued that the rising consumption of goods and services by the developing world will create a very large demand. Consequently, gains would be turned into increased production rather than decreased labor input.

Effects of Government Policy on Innovation

Innovation seems to be very sensitive to a variety of governmental policies. Thus, when exploring the potential impacts of new laws and regulations, Congress needs to be sensitive to possible unintended effects on the innovative process. For example:

- *Taxation:* Industrial investment in innovation is very sensitive to tax policies, particularly those that encourage or discourage capital formation for new firms, for R&D expenditures, and for investments in new processes and equipment.
- *Antitrust:* The purpose of antitrust enforcement is presumably to encourage competition and, hence, innovation. Some experts hold, however, that major antitrust actions or threats of such actions against companies that are large principally because of a successful record of innovation may dampen their enthusiasm for further product development.
- *Regulation:* Regulation can encourage or discourage innovation depending on how it is applied. Regulators either try to direct innovation toward particular societal needs (as in the cases of automotive safety or environmental protection), or to control it for social protection (as in the cases of food and drug safety). The second order effects of this innovation can dampen innovation elsewhere as industrial investment must first respond to the regulatory demand. Only the remaining capital is available for investment.
- *International controls:* Multinational restrictions on the flow of data and computing hardware across national boundaries affect the design of communication-based information systems, and to some extent shape the nature of competition in the international marketplace.
- *Standards:* Federal standards,* voluntary or mandatory, directed at Government or private sector applications can also shape the nature of innovation and competition. On the one hand, for example, some argue that standards for data processing compatibility will encourage a competitive industry to develop around so-called "plug-compatible equipment" (independently manufactured devices that plug into computers

*For a detailed discussion of standards, see app. C to U.S. Congress, Office of Technology Assessment, *Telecommunication Technology and Public Policy,* in press.

made by major firms such as IBM). On the other hand, the premature imposition of standards can freeze the technology at an early stage and inhibit the development of new products and ideas.

What the United States does on its own here may become moot in the longer term. International data standards are developing rapidly. In the United States, the National Bureau of Standards has coordinated the U.S. position. The objective of the International Standards Organization is to have, before the end of the 1980's, compatible protocols and interfaces to allow any one computer to "talk" to any other. Within the United States, pressure in this direction is being exercised through the mandatory Federal Information Processing Standards for Federal Government procurement.

The Federal Communications Commission is presently struggling with the problem of videotext.* Many broadcasters and manufacturers have repeatedly maintained that they cannot invest in developing hardware and services to support such service until they get a clear message on standards. Others argue that the technology is so new that standards at this time could inhibit new developments.[10] In short, the relationship between standards and innovation is not well understood, and could benefit from further study.

*Videotext and related services are systems for providing magazine-like information sources directly over the household television set.

[10]"Upstart Television: Postponing a Threat," *Science* vol. 210, Nov. 7, 1980, pp. 611-615.

Chapter 7
Privacy

Contents

TABLE

Chapter 7
Privacy

Historical Context

Policy issues related to privacy date back many years before the existence of computers.[1] Such issues as the following have long concerned Congress and the Courts:

- Government intrusion—the right of the Government to physically intrude on the premises or in the belongings or personal effects of an individual.
- Surveillance of communication—the right of the Government to intercept communication by reading mail and monitoring telegraph traffic, by wiretapping telephone conversations, or by inspecting envelope exteriors to make a record of the senders (mail covers).
- Liability v. the first amendment—the right of authors to write—and publishers to print—within very broad limits, any information about a person or institution, whether such information is true or false, authorized or not.
- Privileged communication—the right of the Government to seek information conveyed under certain special circumstances, such as psychiatric treatment, religious confession, legal counseling, or media news-gathering.

These examples not only convey the historical nature of privacy debates but also the extraordinary range of issues encompassed by the term.

Privacy as it relates to computers has been more narrowly construed. Historically, the principal discussion has been concerned with computerized banks of information about individuals, the collection of such data, and the uses made of it. A chronology of major events in the development of policy on recordkeeping practices is shown in table 6. In addition, a number of influential hearing records and reports have been issued by Congress.

Recordkeeping has not been the only area of privacy that has concerned Congress. Over the last two decades, hearings have also been held on subjects such as wiretapping, psychological testing of Government

Table 6.—Significant Milestones in the Development of the Recordkeeping Issue[a]

C. 1964	Proposal for a National Statistical Center and the resulting public debate on privacy and Government data systems—culminating in a series of congressional hearings.
1967	Alan Westin's influential book *Privacy and Freedom*.[b]
1970	Fair Credit Reporting Act—provisions regarding credit records on individuals.[c]
1971	Arthur R. Miller's book *The Assault on Privacy: Computers, Data Banks, and Dossiers*.[d]
1972	National Academy of Sciences report: *Databanks in a Free Society*.[e]
1973	Health, Education, and Welfare Secretary's Advisory Committee on Automated Personal Data Systems report: *Records, Computers, and the Rights of Citizens*.[f]
1974	Family Educational Rights and Privacy Act controlling access to educational records.[g]
1974	Privacy Act of 1974 enacted.[h]
1977	Privacy Protection Study Commission report: *Personal Privacy in an Information Society*.[i]
1978	Right to Financial Privacy Act of 1978 enacted to provide controls on release of bank information.[j]

[a]Note: There were also numerous hearings and reports by Senate and House congressional committees during this period, which are not listed here. James Rule and collaborators list 60 major Committee hearings and reports dealing with information privacy from 1966 to 1977.[k]
[b]Alan Westin, *Privacy and Freedom*, New York Atheneum, 1967.
[c]Fair Credit Reporting Act, 15 U.S.C. 1681 (1970).
[d]Arthur R. Miller, *The Assault on Privacy: Computers, Data Banks, and Dossiers* (Ann Arbor: University of Michigan Press, 1971).
[e]Alan Westin and Michael Baker, *Databanks in a Free Society*, (New York: Quadrangle/New York Times Book Co., 1972).
[f]Department of Health, Education, and Welfare, Secretary's Advisory Committee on Automated Personal Data Systems, *Records, Computers and the Rights of Citizens*, Washington, D.C., 1973.
[g]Public Law 93-568.
[h]Public Law 93-579.
[i]Privacy Protection Study Commission, *Personal Privacy in an Information Society*, Washington, D.C., 1977.
[j]Right to Financial Privacy Act of 1978 (Public Law 95-630).
[k]James Rule, et al., *The Politics of Privacy* (New York: Elsevier-North Holland, 1980).

SOURCE: Office of Technology Assessment.

[1]David J. Seipp, *The Right to Privacy in American History*, Harvard University Program on Information Resources Policy, P-78-3, 1978.

employees, and the use of polygraphs. Privacy issues have also been raised by congressional committees concerned with the data systems run by various agencies, in particular the Federal Bureau of Investigation (FBI), the Internal Revenue Service (IRS), the Social Security Administration (SSA), and the Census Bureau.

Privacy-related issues will remain on the congressional agenda over the coming decade for a number of reasons.[2]

- new computer and communication technologies will create new problems and change the nature of old ones;
- the public's awareness of and sensitivity to the privacy problems presented by large data systems appear to remain high; and
- the Federal Government has deliberately chosen to react to privacy issues associated with recordkeeping on a case-by-case rather than on an omnibus basis.

[2]L. Hoffman (ed.), *Computers and Privacy in the Next Decade* (New York: Academic Press, 1980).

Future Privacy Issues

An Omnibus v. A Selective Policy

Omnibus legislation, which would cover all data systems both public and private in which personal information is maintained, is the approach European nations have taken. In the United States this approach has been rejected by the Privacy Commission and the executive branch for several reasons. First, there would be serious difficulties in drafting such legislation in a way that would achieve the desired protection without seriously hampering legitimate data processing applications. Furthermore, the variety of systems, of applications, and of environments, ranging from large banks and insurance companies to street corner drugstores and individual homes, would be hard to accommodate with any single piece of legislation.

In addition, omnibus legislation could lead to the creation of another Federal regulatory agency that would exercise oversight over the information industry. Again, because of the wide variety of applications such an agency would find itself involved in most aspects of American life. The Swedish experience is often given as an illustration. In that much smaller country, a newly created data bank licensing board had 20,000 applications to process in its first year of operation.

With the selective approach, however, Congress will be considering a long series of privacy bills. A substantial legislative effort will be required to catch up with current computerized recordkeeping practices. An immediate concern is the development of privacy rules for computer applications in banking, medicine, social and medical research, credit, insurance, and criminal justice. Privacy is also likely to be a major issue in the development of electronic mail.

Furthermore, new applications for computers and communications, such as an automated securities exchange, in-home information services, electronic publishing, and the automated office, may create new environments for privacy policy issues to arise. As Government agencies such as the Department of Justice, IRS, or SSA begin to use the new generation of information technology for their recordkeeping activities, privacy problems that were not specifically addressed in previous legislation may have to be dealt with by Congress. Recently, for example, the availability of low-cost data communication technology has raised the message-switching issue to prominence in the congressional debate over the future of the operations of the FBI's National Crime Information Center Computerized Criminal History system.

Unlike the executive branch, which can subject all proposed privacy legislation to a consistent agency review, Congress considers the different bills in a variety of committees depending on the applications and users under consideration. Therefore, careful coordination and the adoption of principles for guiding the nature of Federal policy concerned with the handling of personal information in automated information systems is needed in order to prevent the enactment of a patchwork of contradictory privacy legislation.

This approach leads to legislation tailored to the needs of the specific sector affected by it. However, there are also hazards. A danger inherent in disorganized privacy legislation is that businesses that operate in areas of overlapping authority would face a variety of regulations, some even contradictory, governing their data systems. Others might be able to find loopholes by operating in the gray areas between regulated sectors, thereby seriously abusing the intent of Congress.

Because the selective approach differs so radically from the approach taken by most other developed nations, problems could arise internationally. Many developed nations, for example those in the Organization for Economic Cooperation and Development, are attempting to coordinate their privacy legislation so that differences in their rules and practices will not hamper the exchange of information across their borders (see ch. 12). The rejection of an omnibus approach, coupled with the lack of a centralized authority over data banks, is making it difficult for the United States to enter into these international agreements. Such a divergence could leave the United States as "odd man out" with respect to transborder data flow. This could have serious implications for trade and international relations and warrants serious attention.[3]

[3]Donald Marchand, "Privacy, Confidentiality and Computers: National and International Implications of U.S. Information Policy," *Telecommunications Policy,* September 1979, pp. 192-208.

Collection of Data

In an attempt to decrease the amount of data collected by Government agencies, Congress specified in the Privacy Act of 1974 that data collected must be "relevant" to the purposes of the collection. The Privacy Protection Study Commission reported finding a slight decrease in data collection following this legislation.

However, the relevancy test is undeniably weak and difficult to enforce, and the small decrease found in data collection was a one-time phenomenon. Recordkeeping is increasing, both in the Government and in the private sector. Furthermore, as more and more transactions in the private sector become automated, data that would normally not have been collected or retained will now be entered into computer systems and stored, thus becoming available to data collectors.

The recent dispute between Prudential Insurance and the Department of Labor (DOL) over access to personnel tapes is illustrative.[4] To investigate possible discrimination in hiring, DOL has requested complete personnel records held by Prudential. Without judging the merits of the case, it can still be observed that, were the files in question not integrated on magnetic tapes, DOL would have been unlikely to make such a sweeping request because of the burdensome task of analyzing manual records. It should also be noted that computer technology allows such files to be easily processed to create new tapes containing only the information DOL and Prudential would mutually agree is pertinent.

Relevancy is also a weak requirement with respect to its application to the timeliness of data. The Privacy Commission found that agencies were not particularly inclined to cull their files. As the cost of memory continues to drop and very large data systems become easier to operate, even existing economic and managerial incentives to clear

[4]"Prudential Barred From U.S. Contracts," *The Washington Post,* July 29, 1980, sec. A, p. 1.

data bases of old and useless information disappear.

A fundamental assumption underlying much of the privacy debate in the 1970's was that collecting personal information is in the nature of a transaction—the individual yields personal information in exchange for some benefit. Thus, much of the fair practice doctrine centers on the requirement that the recordkeeper abide by obligations implicit in that transaction. However, individuals will increasingly be encountering computerized systems that collect and store information about them without their knowledge or consent. Very few laws exist pertaining to the ownership or disposition of such information, even when its use may be contrary to the individual's perception of his or her best interests.

The mailing list systems were among the involuntary systems studied in depth by the Privacy Commission. Persons have no idea whether or how information about themselves is being compiled. Since, at the time of the study, the Commission deemed mail solicitation to be a socially benign activity, they did not consider this type of recordkeeping to be of serious concern.

However, pressures from users of such systems for greater selectivity in their mailing lists has led to collection of more personal data on individuals. Political solicitation lists, for example, may contain information about a person's organizational affiliations, religious beliefs, charitable contributions, income, and history of support for various causes. This type of information can be used to predict the likelihood that a person would support a particular candidate or political cause and is, therefore, useful in compiling a targeted mailing list.

Such personal information, which is often collected without the consent of the subject through the exchange or purchase of mailing lists or access to other open sources of information, assumes the character of a political dossier. It is not clear that existing controls, either over the use of such data systems for purposes beyond computing mailing lists or over the original collection of the information, are adequate to deal with the increasing capability modern technology offers to collect data and compile such lists.

Modern computer technology through the 1980's will facilitate the collection of personal data, as well as make possible its instantaneous nationwide distribution. Point-of-sale systems are an example of this trend. A sale made at a store and recorded through a terminal will collect a variety of information about a customer, such as what was purchased, the exact time and location of the transaction, and possibly the customer's financial status. This will not only be recorded at the bank, and thus fall under bank privacy rules, but may also be retained by the store management for its own use, or perhaps even sold to third parties.

Access

The controls in current privacy legislation that concern access to Government-held data by other agencies depend on a "use" rule. That is, with some exceptions, data may not be given to a third party for any purpose other than one "compatible" with that for which such data were originally collected. Such routine uses must be made known to the data subject either at the time the data is solicited from him or constructively through publication in the Federal Register.

The Privacy Protection Study Commission found this rule to be relatively ineffective. The word "compatible" is vague and subject to a variety of agency interpretations. In addition, there are a host of exceptions, both within the Privacy Act and in other laws, governing the ways in which agencies exchange information. The provision of notice was found to be equally ineffective. Finally, privacy rules conflict with freedom of information laws. For example, Iowa's attorney general recently ruled that the State's open records laws superseded any rights to user privacy with respect to library records.[5]

The proliferation of personal data collection without either the subject's permission or knowledge implies that even if such a use provision were extended to the private sector and its ambiguities clarified, its effectiveness would be limited. The rule assumes a voluntary relationship between the primary data collector and the subject, and a willing yielding of personal information. Where such an agreement does not exist, the subject of the data is not the "owner" of the information.

The data collector argues, usually correctly, that the information being collected is already in the public domain. The issue may boil down to the difficult question of whether a compilation of information in the public domain along with statistical inferences drawn from it can become so comprehensive as to constitute an intolerable invasion of an individual's privacy. Some States are already considering bills to restrict the access to public records, in particular to auto licensing data.

OTA's study of the FBI's National Crime Information Center/Computerized Criminal History (NCIC/CCH) record system documents the difficulty in enforcing access rules for very large distributed information systems that serve many users and contain information of value to a variety of people. Even if tight security measures could solve the difficult problem of stopping access by unauthorized persons, no controls within the system can keep the data, once extracted by an authorized user, from being used improperly.

Furthermore, the overlap of authority (in the case of NCIC, between Federal, State, and local agencies), along with the concomitant overlapping assortment of rules and procedures, means that it is very difficult to establish a single consistent policy for accessing and using data.

[5] "Iowa Libraries Fight Scrutiny of Borrower Records," *The Washington Post*, Dec. 2, 1979.

This problem is duplicated in the private sector. Retailers of personal data, such as credit bureaus or mailing list operators, have no control over how the information they sell is used. Large corporate information systems, where many employees or even outside users have access to the data, will have similar problems of control.

The question is not just the adequacy of the security of the internal system against unauthorized use, but who is authorized access to the data and how they use it. Many new information systems are characterized by their wide distribution and easy accessibility over communication lines. In fact, they are designed for just these characteristics. In such complex environments, with multiple data bases in the system and multiple users accessing it from anywhere in the Nation, procedural control of data use could be almost impossible.

A final access problem, suggested above, is the impact on privacy of the computerization of traditionally public Government files. Lists of property transfers, licenses, births, deaths, and so on have always been open, but difficult to get at and use. Certainly, they have not been easily absorbed into privately held data bases. Computerized files have changed that access capability, and as a market for such information develops the interest in using it will likely increase.

Microprocessors and Surveillance

The potential now exists for the development and marketing of a wide variety of devices either specifically designed or capable of being used for the surveillance of individuals without their consent. Microprocessor technology is progressing to the point where it will be common for computer logic and data storage capability to be built into inexpensive consumer goods of all kinds. Pocket-size, voice-stress "lie detectors" are already being marketed, although their reliability is unproven. Within a few years, wristwatch-size units will be available. Although at least one State, Pennsylvania, has a law requiring subject consent for use of such devices, its enforcement would be quite difficult when the possession and use of a unit can be so easily hidden.

Currently available security systems based on magnetic cards and microprocessor-based locks allow an employer or building manager to keep detailed records of the whereabouts of anyone in the building. Devices called "pen registers" provide a similar capability for monitoring telephone traffic. If voice recognition and picture processing capabilities improve as much as some experts expect over the next decade, other forms of inexpensive automated surveillance will also become available.

Abuse of this technology for illicit purposes may become a serious problem. However, seemingly legitimate applications such as retail market surveillance of customers or employer surveillance of employees may also cause concern if there are obvious abuses. Arguments for socially sanctioned uses will raise, in new forms, classic issues of civil rights v. both law enforcement and the rights of employers to monitor their employees. In this debate, the new information technology places powerful new tools in the hands of those who argue for greater social control.

The Glass House Society

The issues that are likely to remain active during the next decade or two arise from the public's misgivings that the use of large data systems containing personal information is threatening to them. Recent polls have shown a steadily rising concern over privacy, which is directed equally at Government and private data systems.[6]

Some social and political scientists suggest that the computer represents to the public the growing power of Government and other large organizations over their daily lives.[7] Thus, as the use of these information systems grows, the public's apprehension is also expected to grow as will pressures on public officials to control or even to stop certain types of computer applications.

There appears to be a trend toward a society in which information about a person's finances, medical and educational histories, habits as a consumer, daily movements, and communications with others through the telephone or the mail will be collected, stored in a computer, possibly sold to others, and used in ways over which the individual may have little or no control. There may be many benefits in terms of the productivity and efficiency of institutions, and in terms of broadened awareness and choices available to individuals as citizens and consumers. But the long-term social and political effects of this trend—beneficial and adverse—are still largely unknown. It seems likely, however, that they will be profound, and will alter how individuals both perceive and relate to the institutions that affect their lives. Consequently, Congress will continue to be a principal forum in which these conflicts will be deliberated and ultimately resolved.

[6] *The Dimensions of Privacy: A National Opinion Research Survey of Attitudes Toward Privacy* (Stevens Point, Wisconsin, 1979) for Sentry Insurance.

[7] James Rule, et al., *The Politics of Privacy* (New York: Elsevier-North Holland, 1980).

Chapter 8
The Security of Computer Systems

Contents

Chapter 8
The Security of Computer Systems

Concern and Need

The security of computer systems, particularly those operated by the Federal Government, has increasingly concerned Congress. Hearings have been held, studies have been published by the General Accounting Office, and legislation has been introduced,[1] all addressing the problem of meeting threats to Federal data installations.

Security concerns have also appeared in congressional reaction to proposals for new advanced information systems by Federal agencies, such as the proposed Social Security system, the Tax Accounting System of the Internal Revenue Service, and the upgrading of the National Crime Information Center (NCIC) system of the Federal Bureau of Investigation. All of these proposals have been scrutinized carefully by congressional committees, with particular emphasis on the security of the systems.

Similar concerns have also been expressed by the executive branch. Presidential Directive 24, published in February 1979, established policy for the security of Federal communications and assigned responsibility for the protection of nonmilitary but sensitive Government communications. This directive was motivated by a concern for national security, that is, the potential value of intercepted communications to an enemy.

In a 1978 memorandum,[2] the Office of Management and Budget directed all Federal agencies to pay attention to the security of their data processing operations. The memorandum required the agencies to conduct risk analyses of the threats and vulnerabilities of their systems and to develop appropriate security plans.

The National Bureau of Standards, under authorization by the Brooks Act,[3] is continuing to develop guidelines and standards in all areas of computer security for use by Federal agencies. The first standard to emerge from this effort is the Data Encryption* Standard for protecting data communications. Its adoption may present difficulties because of the rapidly changing technology and the extraordinarily wide range of types and uses of Federal information systems that would have to be covered.

In the domestic sector, the security problem is growing in importance due to several trends:

- The rapidly increasing quantity of computerized data stored and transmitted over communication networks.
- The increasing value of the data, both as a marketable commodity and as representative of value, for example, as in an electronic funds transfer or an automated stock exchange transaction.
- As has been pointed out, an increasing quantity of personal information is being collected, stored, and transmitted. The security needs of electronic mail or of the NCIC system are motivated, in part, by privacy concerns.

[1]See S. 240 (and H.R. 6192), 96th Cong., "Federal Computer Systems Protection Act of 1979," to prohibit the use, for fraudulent or other illegal purposes, of any computer owned or operated in interstate commerce or by the Federal Government or any financial institution.

[2]Office of Management and Budget; circular A-71, "Responsibilities for the Administration and Management of Automatic Data Processing Activities," transmittal memorandum No. 1, "Security of Federal Automated Information Systems," 1978.

[3]Public Law 89-306.

*Encryption is the coding of a message so it is only understandable to a receiver who knows the secret decoding procedure.

- An organization's operations are becoming more dependent on the reliable, secure functioning of the supporting computer system. A computer failure can close down all sales registers in a department store, the air traffic control system, or all the teller stations in a bank.

The Technology of Security

There is a blend of optimism and pessimism in the computer technology community about the future of computer security problems. On the one side, experts correctly point out that the technology of securing computer systems is improving steadily (see ch. 13). They also maintain that computerized systems, even if not perfectly secure, are often far more secure than the manual systems they replaced.

On the other side two main arguments are advanced. First, since security has not been historically a high-priority goal in the design of information systems, the existence of security technology does not necessarily guarantee its proper application. Security hardware and software are often added as an afterthought rather than integrated into the system from the beginning. Most designers have not been trained to build security into the systems they assemble, since security features can increase the initial cost and operating overhead, and may be burdensome to manage.

The second objection is that advances in the technology of protection may not be adequate to deal with the complex systems now being built. In particular, the present trend towards linking computers into networks that use new communication services, which vastly increases the overall complexity of the resulting systems, presents new and difficult challenges to the designer attempting to build a secure system.

Threats and Targets

Analysts view the security problem in several parts. *Threats* are the possible actions of outside forces that may compromise a system. *Targets* are those points within the system against which an attack may be mounted. Assets are the resources of the system (information, money, goods) that may be lost.

Because of the trends cited, threats against computer systems appear to be on the increase. The transfer of funds electronically is only one case in which the information processed is assuming a significant tangible value. Electronic mail and future systems for trading commodities and securities will also tempt criminals. As the society grows more information oriented, the risk of theft will increase along with the potential payoff for its success. In response, a number of computer scientists have focused their attention on computer security.[4] [5]

Computer crime analysts note a number of types of threats:

- theft;
- sabotage;
- data alteration (i.e., in a credit file);
- blackmail;
- extortion;
- corporate espionage;
- system failure;
- service interruption;

[4]Lance J. Hoffman, *Modern Methods for Computer Security and Privacy* (Englewood Cliffs, N.J.: Prentice Hall, 1977).

[5]Donn B. Parker and Susan N. Nycum, *Computer Abuse and Control Study* (Menlo Park, Calif.: SRI International, March 1979).

- natural hazards (e.g., volcanic eruption, flood); and
- unauthorized disclosure.

Computer literacy is growing and with it a proportionate number of people sufficiently knowledgeable to compromise a computer system. In addition, access to low-cost personal computing systems may provide such criminals with more sophisticated tools. At least one such attack has already been made on the telephone system with the aid of a small in-home computer system. Recently, newspapers reported the alleged use of a small computer by high school students to break into the data banks of several Canadian corporations.[6]

Certain social conditions may increase the threats to computer-based systems. A period of stagnation coupled with high inflation could create economic pressures that might lead to an increase in white-collar insider crime. In addition, some social and political scientists see the possibility of an increase in domestic terrorist activity.[7] Foreign experience has shown that such activity is often directed against computer and communication systems, which the perpetrators assume, often rightly, to be at the heart of organizational operations.

Forewarnings such as these, although based on expert opinion, are at best speculative. Nevertheless, security plans must be developed against potentialities, not just certainties. Thus, the possibility that an increase in certain social pressures could lead to economic and sabotage threats against the coming decade's complex information systems is a significant factor in any security analysis.

While threats to information systems and the potential losses from attacks are clearly increasing, the vulnerability of systems to successful attack is changing in character. In some cases it is improving, in others worsening.

The vulnerability of the system software to intrusion should decrease as operating systems are designed with security as a principal goal. They can be expected to be more immune to compromise than those currently available. Data communication will be better protected, both by its changing basic technology and by the incorporation of cryptographic protection. The language used to query the data base will be designed to more easily isolate users from data that they are not authorized to use. Thus, in the future virtually every component of an information system will have better security technology designed into it.

New vulnerability problems, however, will arise at the level of the overall system. As a system becomes larger and more complex, so do the managerial and technical problems of securing it at a system level. The trend toward linking a large number of computer systems together to be used for diverse applications by many persons, scattered geographically, poses system design and management problems that are orders of magnitude larger than those faced in the design of previous generations of information systems. It will be difficult to assess the vulnerability of such complicated systems to accidental or deliberate misuse or failure. Detecting that an untoward incident has occurred would be even more difficult in such systems because of the high volume of work that flows through them and the lack in many systems of full transaction logs.

Although the individual communication links may be more secure (say through encryption), data communication adds its own problems when integrated into information systems. A network of computers that links together individual computer systems over telecommunication lines has numerous points that need to be protected in an environment where failure or penetration at any point compromises the entire system. In addition, such systems are deliberately designed to distribute access, to make it easier

[6] "The Great Dalton School Computer Tie-In Mystery," *New York Times,* July 7, 1980, p. 2, col. 1.

[7] Donn B. Parker, "The Potential Effects of Electronic Funds Transfer on National Security," *Proceedings of the Fifth International Conference on Computer Communication,* October 1980, pp. 470-476.

for users to get at the system, and to decentralize administrative control of the data processing. Consequently, security management—setting up and overseeing administrative and personnel controls—becomes more difficult, both because of the increased number of persons with direct access to the system and because of the geographical dispersion of the organizations involved.

Problems of overlapping or inadequate authority can complicate attempts to control a system's security. This would be the case, for example, with a Federal system that links with State systems, because different nodes in the system would have different rules, practices, and assignments for system security. Yet to be most effective, controls over data access, usage, and security must be applied uniformly over an entire system. A private industry information system that linked together data processing nodes under different authorities would face similar problems.

The problems of controlling access in a widely distributed data network are exemplified by NCIC. (They are discussed in detail in OTA's NCIC assessment, in progress.)

Future Security Issues

Among the several difficult issues involving computer security that are likely to confront Congress over the next decade, the following appear to be the most significant.

Protection of Federal Systems

Federal information systems control the disbursement of an enormous amount of money. The Social Security system itself disburses over $1.5 billion per week. Other Federal systems contain information that could be used directly or indirectly to make profitable financial decisions, e.g., information concerning Federal monetary policy, commodity markets, energy resource estimates, and the like. Still others contain sensitive information relating to personal privacy or national security. All would be highly attractive to theft, manipulation, or eavesdropping.

There are many potential victims of security failures. Taxpayers would suffer the losses from a fraudulent drain on the Federal Treasury. Other types of attacks, for example on social service systems, could create severe hardship for individuals dependent on those programs. In an extreme case, the national security could be threatened, not only by attacks on military and diplomatic computers but also by assaults on such major domestic activities as the air traffic control system or the computer-controlled national electric power distribution grid, whose disruption could create significant social turmoil. Electronic mail service or an electronic funds transfer network would be similarly vulnerable.

Theft, eavesdropping, and sabotage are not the only threats to Federal computer systems that Congress will need to consider. A more subtle threat is a system's potential diversion by the bureaucracy from its intended use. This issue is raised in OTA's NCIC assessment. Expressing similar concern in a different area, Congress has imposed criminal sanctions for bureaucratic violations of the Privacy Act of 1974.[8]

The technology currently available is not very useful for securing a system against this type of bureaucratic abuse, although the researchers in the field of electronic data processing auditing are looking at related problems. Many abuses do not involve violations of the computational procedures within the computer system, but rather represent misuse of the data once it is out of the system. Thus, the most effective controls

[8]Public Law 93-579.

against bureaucratic abuse for now will likely be in the areas of policy, personnel, and management, rather than technical. Strong criminal sanctions for misusing a system may also have a deterrent effect.

As the Government continues to automate, problems of bureaucratic accountability and the responsibility for oversight will confront Congress with the need to better understand and more closely monitor the use of large Federal information systems.

Protection of Vital Domestic Information Systems

There are a number of national interests that will cause Congress to become concerned about the security of major non-Federal national information systems.

Regulations regarding the flow of personal information are proliferating in nations around the world. To date, most laws concern the transfer of personal information and stem from national privacy laws. However, there seems to be a distinct trend toward the extension of these laws to organizations, which are designated as "legal persons"[9] and thus included under privacy laws designed to protect personal data. There is also a growing concern expressed by some nations, particularly those in the Third World, that information originating within their borders is a national resource over which they want to maintain control.[10]

These trends may create additional fears about the security of networked systems that communicate beyond their boundaries. The relatively mild wording about security in current privacy legislation could reappear in much more stringent form in new legislation.

There is also a Federal responsibility for certain information systems that although privately operated, are fundamental to social well-being. The security and reliability of automated systems for nationwide bank check clearing, for a national stock exchange, and for computer-based commodity trading, for example, would all be under the purview of Congress. The vulnerability of such systems is of governmental concern because of the harm that a major system failure could cause to the Nation's economy and to its citizens.

The continuing evaluation of the privacy issue will undoubtedly lead to more stringent security provisions consistent with the evolution toward more communication-based computer systems.

If there is in fact a growing commercial market in personal data, an illicit traffic in stolen information could develop, thus increasing the threat of piracy of personal data from these systems. This would call for tougher and more specific standards for their security.

The Federal Government, due to its traditional concern for the protection of military and diplomatic communications, has a high degree of expertise in the field of data security. A good deal of this expertise is either classified or in the hands of highly sensitive organizations such as the National Security Agency. The appropriate role of the Federal Government has not been defined in transferring this knowledge, for supporting computer security in both the public and private sectors, for setting standards, and for certifying security technology.

The lack of such policy definition is visible in the current debate over Government control of cryptographic technology.[11] In this debate, the needs of the private sector for increased communication security, and hence for the existence of a civilian commercial cryptographic capability, are set against the

[9]H. P. Gassman, "Privacy Implications of Transborder Data Flows: Outlook for the 1980s," *Computers and Privacy in the Next Decade,* L. J. Hoffman, (ed.) (New York: Academic Press, 1980).

[10]American Federation of Information Processing Societies, Panel on Transborder Data Flow, *Transborder Data Flows,* Washington, D.C., 1979.

[11]David Kahn, "Cryptography Goes Public," *Foreign Affairs,* vol. 58, No.1, fall 1979, pp. 141-159.

perceptions of the defense community that such development threatens national security concerns by putting sensitive information in the public domain.[12] A related issue is the desire in the academic community for the freedom to conduct research on the mathematics underlying cryptography.

[12] "Study Group Agrees to Voluntary Restraints," *Science*, vol. 210, Oct. 31, 1980, pp. 511-512 and "MIT Committee Seeks Cryptography Policy," *Science*, vol. 211, Mar. 13, 1981, pp. 1,139-1,140.

Chapter 9
Government Management of Data Processing

Contents

Chapter 9
Government Management of Data Processing

Government Use of Information Technology

In the early days of computing, the Federal Government as a user was a principal stimulus to the development of the field. Agencies such as the Census Bureau, the Bureau of Standards, the Atomic Energy Commission, and the Department of Defense supported the design, programing, and uses of the most sophisticated computer systems in the world. In many cases, development work funded by the Government was carried out in university and industrial laboratories.

A few instances of Federal expertise at the leading-edge of computer applications remain, for example in the scientific research field. However, it appears that, in general, the Federal Government is rapidly falling behind the private sector in its use and management of up-to-date computing technology. If this observation is correct such a lag would penalize Government operations in two ways.

1. *potentially lost opportunities* to use the newest technology to improve the efficiency and effectiveness of Government programs, and
2. *increased cost and decreased reliability* resulting from operating systems that are becoming obsolete, from archaic management procedures, and from burdensome procurement restrictions.

Cheaper computing hardware, the emergence of data communication-based systems, and new software techniques are changing the way computers are used in industry. The next 10 years will see significant movement in the private sector toward automating the flow of information in offices, toward experimenting with new management structures based on high-volume data communication, and toward automating decision support systems for use by higher management. To the extent that these applications fulfill their promise of improvement in both the quality and productivity of management, the Federal Government would be remiss in not making use of them where appropriate.

Government, to a great extent, resembles the service and information sectors of the economy with respect to the role of information technology in making productivity improvements. Any significant productivity improvements brought about by this technology would have to be examined in the light of their possible effects on:

- employment, particularly at the clerical and lower management levels; and
- requirements for training to upgrade or reorient the skills of employees forced to use information technology or displaced by its adoption.

Problems

A host of new demands for Government recordkeeping requirements may arise, ranging from draft registration to the possible expansion of Federal health-care benefits. Increased demands are being made on existing systems, such as that of the Social Security Administration, due to population growth, the increased complexity of the programs that must be administered, and the demand for higher productivity by the bureaucracy.

New information technology will help to provide the tools to meet these needs.

There are indications suggesting that the Government is now experiencing severe difficulties managing the computer technology it currently has in place. The General Accounting Office (GAO) reports, congressional hearings, the report from the recent Presidential reorganization project, personal testimony from Federal electronic data processing administrators, and OTA's assessment of the National Crime Information Center (NCIC) run by the Federal Bureau of Investigation (FBI), all indicate that, for a variety of reasons, the Federal Government does not seem to be managing its computing resources effectively.

A sampling of over 200 GAO reports on electronic data processing (EDP) that have been published over the last few years show the following titles:

- *Federal Productivity Suffers Because Word Processing Is Not Well Managed,* April 1979.
- *Problems Found With Government Acquisition and Use of Computers From November 1965 to December 1977,* March 1977.
- *Contracting for Computer Software Development—Serious Problems Require Management Attention To Avoid Wasting Additional Millions,* November 1979.
- *Inadequacies in Data Processing Planning in the Department of Commerce,* May 1978.
- *IRS Can Better Plan For and Control Its ADP Resources,* June 1979.

The Federal data processing project of the President's reorganization project reported in April 1979 that, while there was a clear need for using advanced information technology, the Government was seriously mismanaging its existing data processing. The OTA assessment of the FBI's NCIC system shows that it has been obsolete for several years and is growing more costly and unreliable to operate. (A recently approved upgrade is now being implemented.) Other studies have shown that the ratio of personnel to hardware costs at Federal installations is nearly twice that of private industry.

Among the reasons proposed for these problems are:

- *Bureaucratic red tape:* Computer technology is changing rapidly; however, the rules governing the procurement and management of automated data systems are proliferating. Unless they are written with technological farsightedness, they can restrict the modernization of an installation's operations. The numbers shown in table 7, which have been taken from a 1977 report of the Office of Management and Budget (OMB),[1] illustrate the welter of rules under which the Federal computing centers operate.
- *Organizational inflexibility:* Recent research has shown that modern information systems profoundly affect the deci-

[1]Office of Management and Budget, *Federal Data Processing Policies and Regulation—Annotated Bibliography,* December 1978.

Table 7.—Policies and Regulations Concerning Federal Data Processing

- 4 laws
- 3 Executive orders
- 3 Presidential memoranda
- 10 Office of Management and Budget circulars
- 12 Office of Telecommunication Policy circulars
- 3 Federal management circulars
- 3 Federal procurement regulations
- 3 Federal Property Management Regulations (FPMR's)
- 16 FPMR bulletins
- 2 FPMR temporary regulations
- 6 National Communication System Guidance Publications
- 60 Federal Information Processing Standards Publications (FIPS Pubs)
- 11 Federal Telecommunications Standards (some overlap with FIPS Pubs)
- 11 Policy letters and memoranda
- 2 Department of Justice Office of Legal Counsel Opinions
- 3 Federal Communications Commission decisions
- 5 General Services Administration Management Guidance Documents

SOURCE: Office of Management and Budget, 1977.

sionmaking patterns in organizations.[2] The research suggests that computerized information systems are particularly effective under special conditions; these depend on the operational level and support for the system. At higher levels of organizations, information systems are more subject to the politics and conflicts of organizational life. While at times these systems prove to be effective, at other times they will be unworkable because existing powerful groups will not cooperate in systems development and use. Experience in the private sector likewise suggests that attempts to force major new information systems into rigidly traditional and unreceptive management structures are often doomed to failure.[3] Yet, reorganizing a bureaucracy is a difficult and highly political process.

- *Procurement delays:* Federal EDP managers complain that the procurement process is so complex, confusing, and fraught with delay that by the time a new systems concept is actually realized in the installation of new hardware, the system is already approaching obsolescence. Estimates of delays in the procurement process for some large systems run as long as 6 years, long enough for the desired technology to become obsolete. Estimates do not include the further delays imposed by discussions within the executive branch or Congress of the appropriateness of the systems or of their possible social impacts.
- *Staffing problems:* There has been some concern expressed that Government computer expertise itself has been growing obsolete. In particular, the Government has trouble competing with private industry for highly talented, and correspondingly expensive, programing and systems analysis talent.

  Furthermore, although job-hopping and staff turnover have been chronic problems for private industry, this rotation also seems to produce a cadre of very broadly experienced, expert, and up-to-date programers in the labor pool. Not only do these people learn faster, but as they change jobs they bring new ideas and techniques into each data processing center. Government programing staff seems to be more static, moving less between agencies and almost never between private industry and the Government.

  In addition, a principal drawing card for talented programers is the opportunity to work on state-of-the-art systems. The job of maintaining a decade-old operating system on an out-of-date computer, even if very highly paid, is unlikely to attract an experienced and talented programer. Thus, the obsolescence of Federal systems sets up a vicious circle—a disincentive to the kind of people who could best develop new systems.
- *Debates over social impacts:* The installation of several large, new data processing systems has been delayed or, in some cases, completely halted in the face of congressional concerns about impacts these systems might have on constitutional rights and other societal values such as privacy. Plans proposed for integrated Federal data banks have also occasioned public debate. Thus, it is reasonable to assume that there will be a great deal of social sensitivity and distrust or at least wariness about major new data systems. This concern will affect particularly those applications that are designed to handle personal data.

It may be that a more clearly articulated set of social policy concerns with more concrete guidelines will aid Federal agencies to better anticipate the questions of societal

[2] R. Kling and W. Scacchi, "Computing as Social Action, the Social Dynamics of Computing in Complex Organizations," *Advances in Computers,* vol. 19 (New York: Academic Press, 1980).

[3] Henry C. Lucas, *Why Information Systems Fail* (New York: Columbia University Press, 1975).

impacts before they arise. Furthermore, system managers and designers working in these agencies need to be more sensitive to these broader policy concerns, which can run counter to more narrow engineering design goals such as efficiency and reliability.

Issues

There seems to be no doubt that several major new data processing systems will be needed by Federal agencies within this decade. Congress will, therefore, be faced with a number of problems involving planning, designing, procuring, and managing these systems.

Some legislative attempts to rationalize Federal EDP have been made. The most notable is the 1967 amendment, which is known as the "Brooks Act," to the Federal Property and Administrative Services Act. This act set up authorities in the executive branch to regulate agency procurement of data processing equipment. The most recent significant bill was H.R. 6410/S. 1411 passed by Congress and signed into law December 11, 1980. This public law, known as the Paperwork Reduction Act of 1980, establishes central oversight in OMB of the information policies and practices of the executive branch. Perhaps most important, this act emphasizes the basic need for restructuring the way information resources and supporting technologies are managed in the Government. This represents a new approach by giving management of information resources similar importance to that traditionally assigned to managing financial and personnel resources. Many issues and questions need attention from this broader perspective. For example:

- There is a need to better understand the effects of large-scale information systems on the internal organization and management of Government agencies and on decisionmaking in Federal agencies.[4]

[4]K. Laudon, "Privacy and Federal Data Banks," *Society*, January/February 1980, pp. 50-56.

Congress and the public need to know more about location of responsibility, the quality of the decisions, the nature of due process for clients affected by those decisions, and the accountability of the bureaucracy to Congress and to higher-level policymakers in the executive branch. A better understanding of the broader and longer term social impacts of a massive automated bureaucracy is also needed.

Many questions are still unanswered. Can there be both increased efficiency and fairness in Federal data processing? Are there inherent threats to the civil liberties of the clients of agencies that automate their decisionmaking? Will there be more subtle effects on social values and on the political attitudes of citizens toward Government?

Some research on these topics, particularly on managerial effects, has been done in the context of private sector organizations. A few investigators have also started to look at local government impacts.[5]

Some of these results may be directly applicable to Federal agencies; other findings can only be suggestive. For example, research suggests that some local agencies may use their information systems for political purposes rather than to improve administrative efficiency.[6] Single, centralized policy-oriented information systems may not

[5]William Dutton and Kenneth Kraemer, "Management Utilization of Computers in American Local Governments," *Communications of the Association of Computing Machinery*, vol. 2, No. 1, March 1978, pp. 305-309.

[6]Rob Kling, "Automated Welfare Client-Tracking and Service Integration: The Political Economy of Computing," *Communications of the Association of Computing Machinery*, vol. 21, No. 6, June 1978, pp. 484-493.

necessarily be more objective than their manual counterparts (containing less data); much may be gained by having competing systems.[7] While these and other studies of private sector and local government information systems may not shed much light on Federal information systems, this existing body of empirical studies does provide a useful starting place.[8] [9] [10] Careful similar studies of Federal systems should be undertaken, since these systems are often large in scale, accountable to a wider variety of interests, and managed under somewhat different vendor and civil service arrangements.

Little actual research has been done on these broader policy issues, although there is an indication of some activity among analysts working in this field. One possibility would be for some appropriate agency to be encouraged by Congress to support research in the important areas of social impact. Such a program could fund long-term investigations that look beyond the short-range focus of most current policy analysis.[11]

- The process by which appropriate social values and goals are reflected in system design needs clarification. Major new systems will need to be evaluated by Congress for their effects on privacy, security, constitutional rights, and many other issues that are not normally the concern of the designer or operator of an information system.

Four fundamental approaches are available to deal with social value questions:

1. Congress could assess the potential social impacts of each new system design that is proposed on a case-by-case basis.

   There are several dangers inherent in such an approach. Inconsistent policies may be set for different systems and different agencies (or even for different versions of the same systems at different times); the evaluation process can seriously delay procurements; and because the system designer is not aware of which issues will be deemed important and which requirements are likely to be placed on the system, the design is nearly always subject to the criticism that it is seriously deficient.
2. Congress could codify a social impact policy concerning all Federal information processing systems. An appropriate executive branch agency could be designated as responsible for seeing that all new system designs are evaluated in relation to that policy.

   The drawbacks would be the difficulty of developing such a policy in the first place, and the loss of the ability to evaluate each new system in light of its own peculiar characteristics and the specific mission of the operating agency.
3. Congress could continue to examine agency proposals system-by-system, but would base its evaluation on a social impact framework encompassing a set of principles for the design and operation of Federal information systems. This process has already been started by the Privacy Act of 1974, which expressed congressional concern about one specific aspect of Federal agency recordkeeping practices, the effect on the privacy rights of individual citizens.
4. Proposals for simplifying the procedures for purchasing data processing equipment will probably be introduced in Congress during this decade. It will be necessary for Congress to balance the need to speed up design and pro-

---

[7]Rob Kling, "Information Systems in Public Policy Making: Computer Technology and Organizational Arrangements," *Telecommunications Policy,* vol. 2, No. 1, March 1978, pp. 22-32.

[8]Dutton, and Kraemer, op. cit.

[9]Rob Kling, "Social Analyses of Computing: Theoretical Perspectives in Recent Empirical Research," *Computing Surveys,* vol. 12, No. 1, March 1980, pp. 61-110.

[10]Kling and Scacchi, op. cit. pp. 250-327.

[11]See, for example, H.R. 4326, 96th Cong., to establish a commission on the implications of information technology in education. Also see H.R. 8395 introduced by Rep. George Brown in the 96th Cong., 2d sess. This bill would establish an Institute for Information Policy and Research to address national information policy issues.

> curement of Federal systems, against the paramount requirements that tax money be spent as effectively and as equitably as possible and the necessity to consider carefully the societal impacts of these systems.

Some opponents of large information systems welcome delays as useful impediments to the installation of new information systems that could turn out to be unnecessary or even harmful. However, if after careful consideration Congress approves a particular information system, bureaucratic delay could be viewed as disadvantageous, undermining the potential utility and performance of the system and the effectiveness of the relevant agency.

Chapter 10
Society's Dependence on Information Systems

Contents

Chapter 10
Society's Dependence on Information Systems

Introduction

The nature of risk is being changed by much of the new high technology on which modern society depends—jumbo commercial airlines, nuclear powerplants, oil supertankers, or large computer-based information systems. In general, because new technologies can be designed to operate more reliably than the ones replaced, the risk that any particular mechanism may fail has been reduced. However, should an accidental or deliberate disruption occur, its cost can be much larger, even catastrophic. Furthermore, when society becomes highly dependent on the reliable functioning of single integrated technological systems or small collections of such systems, the possibility of a "domino-like" collapse of several of the individual connected units could also be disastrous. The failure of the Northeast power grid in 1965, which blacked out much of that section of the United States including all of New York City, is an example.[1]

Integrated systems are often created by information technology. There has been a strong historical trend toward connecting components over communication lines to form complex distributed systems, while at the same time computers have become smaller and more dispersed. In OTA's examination of future technology (see ch. 13), it was concluded that this trend toward integration would continue, driven by the effort to make information systems more convenient and more efficient.

When examining technologies such as electronic funds transfer (EFT) systems, widely available electronic mail service (EMS), and other large extensively used information systems, the following should be taken into consideration.

- The ways in which public policy can help to allocate and balance the risks society may encounter from national information systems against the benefits it may receive, under conditions where failure rates appear to be relatively low but potential losses may be high should a failure occur.
- The ability of society to retain the option to end its dependence on a particular information system if it has unanticipated undesirable effects; in other words, to avoid the possibility of becoming "locked in" to the use of certain information systems once they are installed.
- The capability of providing alternatives to persons or institutions choosing not to accept perceived risks in a new information system.
- The ways in which technology can be utilized to reduce the risks, for example by introducing additional system redundancy (alternative paths between points in the system, distributed data bases, backup computers). The risks inherent in U.S. dependence on a nationwide, interconnected telephone system (which itself is rapidly being computerized) are mitigated to a degree by the large number of switching centers and parallel trunklines.

[1] Rob Kling, "Value Conflicts and Social Choice in Electronic Funds Transfer Systems Developments," *Communications of the Association for Computing Machinery,* vol. 21 No. 8, August 1978, pp. 642-657.

Failure

Large complex information systems contain millions of logical connections and are controlled by programs that themselves can be composed of millions of instructions. Consequently, it is difficult to calculate their reliability and to predict the failure rate of any particular part of the system, as well as the effect of a failure on the operation of the entire system. A further complication is that when a major failure does occur, it is often caused by a rare combination of multiple breakdowns of components. It is currently not possible to incorporate all of these probabilities into a single characterization of system reliability.

This failure problem is illustrated by a recent breakdown of the ARPANET, a nationwide packet switched network intended to be and normally regarded as highly reliable.

- The network's builders recognized that component failure is inevitable in any system and designed the network to be tolerant of such failures. The approach taken was to design the network's traffic control algorithms so as to isolate each failure to the processor or other system element in which the failure first occurred.
- The overall success of these algorithms and the software that embodies them is borne out by the rare occurrence of failure conditions that affect any significant portion of the network.
- But a recent failure did occur in the traffic control software itself—the very mechanism intended to minimize the spread of failure. Bad data in one processor was rapidly and systematically propagated throughout the network, bringing traffic to a standstill. Under normal conditions such propagation is necessary and desirable to allow the network to keep track of its current condition. Unfortunately, the propagation of false data, like poison, proved fatal. Thus, the network's primary shield against failure proved to be its Achilles heel.

This example demonstrates how difficult it is to design large and complex systems which are also reliable. Nonetheless, in many situations a distributed system such as ARPANET may be much more reliable than a centralized system of the same size, because of the distributed system's potential for isolating and therefore surviving local failures without a total system breakdown.

Little data exist from which to calculate failure probabilities because of the newness of information technology and its low failure rate. In addition, each system is uniquely designed for its purpose; therefore very little useful experience has been accumulated that would be applicable to calculating the probability of the potential failure rate for large complex systems in general.

The problem of estimating risks under conditions characterized by an uncertain but very low probability of failure and by a very high potential cost of failure has stimulated a burst of new research in risk analysis. The National Science Foundation has initiated a program of research that should contribute to improving the ability to calculate more accurately risks for large systems over the long term.

In addition, attempts are being made to design so-called "robust" systems. These systems have very high reliability, can diagnose failure, and in some cases can even replace failed components by switching to alternative ones. The message-switching computers that are custom-designed for use in the telephone network employ some of these techniques to achieve very high reliability, as do on-board spacecraft computers where long-term reliability is crucial.

It is difficult to carry out risk analysis for integrated information systems for the following reasons:

- Their *complexity,* which makes some design errors inevitable but also makes accurate estimations of system reliability very difficult.
- The *speed of computers,* in which millions of transactions are processed every minute, makes human monitoring virtually impossible. Consequently, system failures can quickly drive the system to a worst-case collapse before any human intervention can take place. This criticism was made during the congressional debate on the antiballistic missile system. It was argued that a system malfunction could fire the missile before any human intervention could detect the error and cancel the action.

  An automated national stock market or centralized check clearing system could also be subject to such catastrophes. Banks or brokerage houses could be ruined in a matter of minutes, long before it was discovered that the system had failed. The potential victims would be the owners of the failed system, individuals with accounts, correspondent organizations, and, were the failure to cascade through other institutions, even all of society.
- *Centralization of data,* which occurs in many large information systems and is partly motivated by the higher security possible with a centralized system. Even if failure rates continue to be as low as predicted, this concentration would greatly increase the size of a potential loss should the very rare event occur.
- *Interconnection between systems* increases their vulnerability to failure by introducing another element, while at the same time providing a connecting path through which a failure at one node can spread to others, as was the case with the power blackout referred to earlier.

  A large, nationally networked information system may provide more day-to-day security by supplying instant backup to nodes that may fail. However, there may be also a greater risk that the entire system will go down in the event of an unlikely or unexpected combination of events.
- *Societal dependence* on the uninterrupted operation of large information systems will increase along with potential societal loss from their failure. The development of these systems is being motivated by the need for assistance in managing the increasingly complex activities of U.S. society and its organizations. These systems then become integral parts of the processes—central to their operation—rather than merely tools.

  This evolution to dependency can be seen already in the reliance of safe public air transport on the continuous operation of the computerized air traffic control system. In the commercial sector, large stores and banks rely on the smooth uninterrupted operation of their centralized computer systems. Future EMS and EFT systems will likely create similar societal dependencies much larger in scale than current examples.

It is not hard to project into the 1980's and envision the potential damage that could be caused by the failure or misuse of such systems as they grow larger, more complex, and more centralized. Some of the risks may be *physical* as in the air traffic control example or with a computerized nuclear reactor safety system. Others may be in the form of *economic* losses, such as the failure of an automated check clearing system or a national automated securities market. Still other risks may be *social,* as would occur if the larger data systems such as the National Crime Information Center or an EFT payment system were misused by the Government or by private concerns to exert undue control over individuals.

Issues

Underlying all of these concerns is the realization that although the probability that any catastrophic event will occur may be low, the potential social cost of such an event can be extremely high—even a threat to national security. This problem of social vulnerability is crucial to many issues that Congress will be addressing relating to information systems.

Specific Systems and Threats

Congress is already confronting these larger social vulnerability issues in the context of particular information systems:

- The air traffic control system has reportedly failed several times, leading to pressures for a new improved system. Possible new systems are being assessed by OTA.[2] An important but difficult question is the degree to which any new system improves reliability.
- Press reports have suggested that the Defense Department's WWMCCS* command and control system is unreliable, particularly when fully loaded under crisis conditions.[3]
- An article in the Washington Post suggests that the defense communication system is highly vulnerable, not only to full-scale nuclear attack, but to sabotage by terrorist groups.[4]

This last instance is the social vulnerability issue carried to the extreme, the vulnerability of a U.S. defense communications network to hostile attack. However, the line demarcating information systems that are vital to national security is difficult to draw, for it may include major civilian domestic systems.

Ever since Soviet interception of U.S. domestic telecommunications was reported, the executive branch has been working toward securing civilian government communications. They have also been concerned with the national security threats to domestic private communications, but the development of a policy has been slow and difficult due to the need to avoid substantial Federal intrusion into the private sector.[5]

Events over the next decade, such as a chilling of relations with foreign adversaries or an increase in domestic terrorism, would focus congressional attention on the vulnerability to attack of nonmilitary facilities such as EFT, EMS, or civilian government data systems.

Calculating Risk

Aside from the national security question, however, Congress will need to consider the societal risks inherent in new information systems. The concern about risk will lead Congress and other policymakers to search for more flexible information technologies to implement, whose failure will not be so devastating to society. Such systems, if they can be developed, may appear to be less efficient or to cost more in the short run, but would reduce the overall vulnerability of society to catastrophe.

Assignment of Risk

In deciding how to define an acceptable risk, the extent to which American society as a whole will or should accept responsibility for losses incurred due to massive failures of information systems must be taken into consideration.

---

[2] U.S. Congress, Office of Technology Assessment, *Assessment of the Airport and Air Traffic Control System*, in progress.

*An acronym for the *World Wide Military Command and Control System*.

[3] William J. Broad, "Computers and the U.S. Military Don't Mix," *Science*, vol. 207, Mar. 14, 1980, pp. 1183-1187.

[4] Joseph Albright, "The Message Gap in Our Crisis Network," *Washington Post*, Oct. 19, 1980, pp. C1, C4.

[5] G. Lipsound, *Private and Public Defenses Against Soviet Interception of U.S. Telecommunication: Problems and Policy Points* (Cambridge, Mass.: Harvard University Center for Information Policy Research, 1979).

In the case of EFT, for example, the question might be whether the Government should insure liability against a major system collapse beyond the level currently provided by the Federal Deposit Insurance Corporation. A national automated securities market would raise similar problems.

When such losses have an extremely low probability, the difficulties associated with assigning risk can be easily put aside. The implication is that the policy decisions will be made on an ad hoc basis only after a failure has occurred. However, the political climate immediately after a major technological failure may not be amenable to making policy that would be sound over the long term and applicable to new events.

Management of Risk

A case can be made that much current Government regulation represents an attempt to manage risk in order to reduce hazards from consumer products, from drugs, from the workplace, or from the natural environment.[6] If national information systems create significant social risks, and if Congress chooses to attempt to mitigate those risks, several possible mechanisms or mixes of mechanisms are available for consideration.

- *Regulation:* Direct management through laws and administrative rules is currently being questioned as an effective means to regulate risk. For example, direct regulation was rejected by the Privacy Commission as an approach to the privacy problem. However, in specific sectors where the industry is already federally regulated, such as banking or securities exchange, Government may choose to directly set policies for protecting information systems.

  The Government is establishing standards for secure design of systems used by Federal agencies. While these standards do not apply directly to the private sector, they could provide incentives for similar design, either by setting a favorable example or by establishing a minimum standard of practice that the courts might recognize in liability suits.

Alternatives to regulations may also be considered. Two that have been proposed are:

1. *Liability:* Liability law is the chief risk deterrent through the legal mechanisms available, e.g., lawsuits.
   - Liability case law is very slow to develop, depending as it does on an accumulation of court decisions and appeals.
   - The message sent to organizations through court decisions can be vague and difficult to interpret. Thus, an unnecessarily conservative approach may be inadvertently encouraged, and promising socially desirable technological innovations may be precluded.
   - The courts can find it difficult to deal with highly complex technical issues in the context of litigation.
   - Liability law varies from State to State, particularly in terms of the ways in which negligence and non-negligence are defined. This creates a climate of uncertainty with respect to how the law will be applied.
2. *Insurance:* While secondary to liability law in importance, insurance is another method of controlling risk by spreading it over a large number of persons or organizations. Its cost is an incentive to the client to reduce risk. This is particularly true where there is a potential for catastrophic loss. In such cases, insurance companies generally require an extremely large deductible and/or impose limited liability ceilings. However, any attempt to turn to insurance as a mechanism to control risk must deal with the following problems:

[6]David Okrent, "Comment on Societal Risk," *Science*, vol. 208, Apr. 25, 1980, pp. 372-395.

- insurance can be discriminatory in ways not deemed to be in the social interest;
- by concentrating on minimizing loss to the insured, broader social losses are ignored or underrated; and
- when the cost of the insurance is not a sufficient deterrent, it can actually encourage persons or organizations to assume risks that are not prudent.

Chapter 11
Constitutional Rights

Contents

Chapter 11
Constitutional Rights

Introduction

Little legal precedent exists, in many cases, for applying constitutional law to the issues raised by computer-based information systems. As the courts begin to deal with the novel issues raised by the application of computer technology, they will probably attempt to apply traditional concepts. In this way, these new issues will become incorporated into existing legal precedent.

Legislative remedies may be called for when the courts do not find constitutional protections for threats to individual rights created by unforeseen technological developments such as television cameras, electronic wiretapping, and computer data banks. It is difficult to predict in advance precisely which computer-raised constitutional issues will create major legislative problems and which will be easily accommodated in the courts. Expert opinions vary widely, and little legal research has been done as yet.

The legal survey task of this study identified five areas of constitutional law that may be affected by information systems. These are:

- first amendment rights, which guarantee freedom of religion, speech, the press, peaceable assembly, and the right to petition for redress of grievances;
- fourth amendment rights, which guarantee against unreasonable search and seizure by the Federal Government;
- fifth amendment rights, which guarantee that a person may not be compelled to be a witness against himself or be deprived of life, liberty, or property without due process of law;
- sixth amendment rights, which guarantee the right of a speedy and public trial; and
- 14th amendment rights, which guarantee that a State cannot deprive any person of life, liberty, or property without due process of law nor deny any person within its jurisdiction the equal protection of the laws.

First Amendment

The principal purpose of guaranteeing freedom of speech is to ensure a free marketplace of ideas. Courts have tended to balance this freedom against other compelling social concerns, e.g., national security or public safety. For example, there have been a number of recent cases about the rights of reporters to protect their sources. However, certain characteristics of specific communication media affect how that goal is achieved.

The *printed page* is the least regulated communication medium. No Government interference in the content of published material is tolerated with the exception of some fairly limited and still contested restrictions in the areas of pornography, national security, libel, and trade practices. The relatively low cost and ubiquity of printing technology usually guarantees universal access to it for those who have something to say.

The *common carriers* are more restricted. Telephone and mail service are regulated monopolies that control the huge capital and institutional structures necessary to carry messages in various forms. Nevertheless, the communication capacity is very large. Without regulation, the potentiality would exist that an operator might restrict a person's access to the medium. Regulation is therefore oriented toward assuring universal access by requiring carriers to provide uniform service to all at regulated prices. As with print, there are no limitations on message content aside from certain restrictions on pornography and other illegal activities.

The *broadcast* medium has a limited number of owners and operators as well as a limited capacity. Regulation must take into account the existence of these inherent restrictions on its use. Consequently, the thrust of the regulation is not the right of all to speak, but rather the right of all to be exposed to a "free market in ideas." Under this interpretation, the Federal Communications Commission (FCC) has actively specified standards for broadcast content in such requirements as the "fairness" doctrine.

Cable services share both broadcast and common carrier characteristics, since their capacity is still limited but much greater than that of broadcast services. FCC, in its early licensing policy, required cable stations to provide public access channels that would be available to any potential user. (This requirement, among others, was rendered moot by a Supreme Court decision restricting FCC's authority to regulate in this area.)[1] If cable providers have local monopolies over the delivery of information services to homes and businesses, there is a public interest in preventing the cable provider from exercising religious, political, or artistic censorship over the content.

Since the nature of first amendment protections is so strongly dependent on the characteristics of the media, it is reasonable to expect that new *information services* of the future will force the development of new types of policy. Some of the significant characteristics that may determine these policies are:

- *Restricted ownership and control of physical facilities.* Very high capital investments are required to install physical communication channels into homes and businesses. Even if competition in providing information services is encouraged, it is likely that there will be relatively few suppliers of facilities,* leaving the control over the physical communication lines to a few large organizations.
- *Much greater capacity.* The capacity of future communication lines into homes and businesses will be much greater than the current telephone and broadcast facilities. Cable and direct satellite broadcast lines will provide more channels and greater information capacity per channel. In addition, communication from the home back to the sender will be possible. Some limited implementations of two-way capability already exist, and expansion is likely over the next decade.
- *More producers.* The larger number of communication channels into the home coupled with low-cost national distribution systems are expected to lead to a proliferation of information producers and distributors beyond the current limited number of television networks.** Services such as those provided by the new "super stations" that operate nationwide over local cable networks, pay television networks such as Home Box Office, and upcoming direct satellite broadcast stations represent only the leading edge of such a trend in the entertainment area. In data communications, MicroNet and The Source are new services designed to link owners of personal computers with each

[1]*Federal Communications Commission* v. *Midwest Video,* 440 U.S. 689, 59 L.E.D. 2d 693, 99 Supreme Court 1435 (1979).

*The actual number of facility suppliers is growing (e.g., specialized common carriers and satellite carriers who supply a significant portion of their own facilities). However, this growth is much slower than that of the information producers.

**The new cable TV systems being built in the United States have up to 50 TV channels; some will have as many as 100 TV channels.

other and with larger computers, data banks, and information processing services over a nationwide network.

- *Low-cost access.* Network broadcasters pay thousands of dollars per minute to generate and transmit information. The new information and communication technology will substantially reduce the cost of distributing information. Therefore, it will be easier to enter the market, and a wider variety of information services will be made available.

The principal first amendment issue facing the Government will be to encourage the maximum freedom of expression—fostering the "marketplace of ideas"—in new electronic media that have been tightly regulated in more traditional forms. Factors that could work against this goal include pressures for Government censorship, monopoly in the production and distribution of certain kinds of programs and services, and excessive control over content by the operator or operators of the physical communication channels.

Another issue may serve to link first amendment rights with privacy concerns. Extensive data collection and possibly surveillance by Government and private organizations could, in fact, suppress or "chill" freedoms of speech, assembly, and even religion by the implicit threats contained in such collection or surveillance.[2] These threats might be directed as much at the "listener" as the "speaker." Clearly, automated information delivery systems possess a much greater capability of recording, storing, and analyzing in detail the flow of information from all sources into homes than do manual systems such as bookstores, newspapers, and the like.

As a consequence, consideration needs to be given to the distinction between information that is regarded by people to be private in nature and that which is public. Such a distinction may depend on whether the use of the information favors or is detrimental to the interests of an individual. For example, one does not usually attempt to keep secret the titles of books borrowed from a public library. However, an accurate profile of an individual's interests and attitudes could be provided by a complete dossier on that person's reading habits. Since computer technology has the potential capability of assembling such data bases, it may necessitate creating new definitions of the boundary between public and private information.

[2]Sam J. Ervin, "The First Amendment: A Living Thought in the Computer Age," *Columbia Human Rights Review,* vol. 4, No. 1, 1972, pp. 13-47.

Fourth Amendment

The fourth amendment protects the persons, houses, papers, and effects of individuals against unreasonable searches and seizures by the Federal Government. The study identified three significant areas in which new computer and communication systems may affect the interpretation and application of the fourth amendment.

1. the use of personal and statistical data contained in automated information systems as a justification for search and seizure;
2. the search and seizure of information per se as personal property, particularly in electronic form; and
3. the use of automated information systems as a tool for search and seizure operations.

Justification for Data Collection

Criminal justice agencies have traditionally kept files that form the basis of their investigations. Depending on the system design, however, automation can change the nature of this recordkeeping in several ways:

- there are more individuals as data subjects;
- there are more data per individual;
- there is more centralization and correlation of diverse data sources;
- there is wider access to the data by more persons;
- there is faster access to the data; and
- there is more efficient remote access to the data.

Using the technology to the fullest capacity, it would be possible within the next decade for a policeman to obtain instantly a complete identification and dossier on an individual stopped in the street. As criminal justice information systems approach this capability, courts will become more interested in questions such as "reasonable cause" for such police actions as stopping and searching an individual. There is also the possibility of using statistical data as a basis for establishing probable cause.

In their concern, courts will probably look at issues of data quality. An erroneous record in a local manual file could cause an individual some distress, but an erroneous or incomplete record in a large, automated system with national or regional access could lead to more serious compromise of individual rights unless the record was promptly corrected.* This consideration combined with other related reasons could motivate courts to mandate that stringent data quality requirements must be met by automated systems before information from them could be used as reasonable cause for criminal justice actions.** In theory, checking and correcting records could be done more quickly with an automated system.

*In addition to the issues arising from the protections guaranteed by the fourth amendment, if access to the system were loosely controlled, and data used for purposes other than criminal justice such as employment or credit, serious harm could result.

**The issue of data quality is explored in more detail in the OTA study on NCIC/CCH, in progress.

Information as an Object of Search and Seizure

The same information and information technology on which most institutions and people in this country increasingly depend for the conduct of their everyday lives are also becoming of greater importance to investigations conducted by the criminal justice system. Files, ledgers, correspondence, and address books have always been the objects of police searches in certain types of crimes. The criminal justice system will increasingly have to deal with their much more extensive computer equivalents, which may well raise new fourth amendment questions.

Two trends serve to increase the exposure of persons to searches. The first is that information previously unrecorded in any form will become collectable in computer data banks; electronic mail and electronic point of sale systems, for example, collect and store more data than the systems they replaced. The second trend is that data previously in the hands of individuals are now collected and stored by third parties, throwing the ownership of such data into question.

In a recent case,* the Supreme Court ruled that an individual's bank records belonged to the bank and were not protected constitutionally as his or her personal property. One basis for this ruling was that the use of a bank account was a voluntary action. Yet, it is questionable whether future participation in a computerized society can be construed to be voluntary if the alternative is to forgo all services necessary to live comfortably as a member of that society. Extensions of such reasoning could leave only a hollow shell of fourth amendment protection for personal records, while eroding any substantive effective barriers against Government intrusion.

As this happens, Congress will be asked to reestablish these protections legislatively. In the above cited case, a congressional act** addressed the problem of protecting

**United States* v. *Miller,* 425 U.S. 435 (1976).

**The Right to Financial Privacy Act (12 U.S.C. 340).

personal records held by financial institutions from access by the Federal Government.

The search and seizure of computerized records will probably present courts and legislatures with a number of problems in balancing the needs of law enforcement with fourth amendment protections. For example:

- When identifying records as objects of search and seizure, traditional standards that were reasonably effective with written documents may not apply when the information sought is buried in a very large, or even geographically distributed, computer data file.
- In its original or primary form, computer data is unreadable by human beings. Thus, seized evidence may be in a primary form, such as magnetic tape or disk, or it may be in a secondary form, such as printouts or charts. The status of this type of evidence may be contestable, particularly if a law enforcement agency is required to perform sophisticated file manipulation in order to pull out the particular information it is trying to introduce as evidence.
- If the information is in coded form (encrypted) and the key to its decoding (decryption) is only in the head of the suspect, fifth amendment protections may allow that person to withhold the encryption/decryption key or the encryption algorithm. Similar problems exist even short of encryption. Information can be hidden in a large data bank in such ways that it would be nearly impossible to find without knowing its precise location.

It is expected that the normal evolution of law in the courts will be able to deal with many of these problems as they occur. However, as the Miller case illustrates, the logical extension of legal principles into the information age can on occasion seriously alter the balance of power between individuals and Government, threatening protections included in the U.S. Constitution and Bill of Rights. In such cases, a legislative remedy will become necessary.

Information Technology as a Tool for Search and Seizure

Despite the difficulties of collating information that is dispersed and buried in very large geographically distributed computer files, national information systems may provide mechanisms for surveillance that penetrate more deeply into an individual's privacy than was previously possible.

In determining when fourth amendment protections apply, law enforcement distinguishes between "surveillance" and "search and seizure." There is no violation of this protection in observing an individual's daily public activity. It is the actual search of a person, a person's premises, or the seizure of personal records that requires warrants.

Information technology blurs the line between public and private activity. A nonelectronic mail cover requires approval by the Postal Inspection Service but not a search warrant because only the outside of an envelope is examined. In an electronic mail system, however, no distinction may exist between the "outside" (or address) and the "inside" (or contents) of a message. Therefore, it may be difficult to distinguish a mail cover from a wiretap, which would require a warrant issued by a court upon probable cause, unless some form of coding could act to "seal" an electronic message as an envelope seals a physical one.

Similarly, the observation of shopping habits by following a person from store to store is surveillance. However, the use of an electronic funds transfer system to gather the same type of information would be far more intrusive, since much more data, some of it of a highly personal nature, could be collected in secret. The question is whether such transactions are to be considered public or private behavior.

The telephone created the possibility of wiretapping, which has stimulated numerous debates balancing the needs of law enforcement against those of individual privacy and fourth amendment protection. The courts and Congress have been struggling for some time with interpretations of the fourth amendment in terms of wiretapping. Information systems that provide such services as electronic mail and electronic funds transfer will likely provoke similar debates in Congress.

There is no doubt that access to computerized information could assist law enforcement in detecting crime and in prosecuting offenders. Consequently, the benefits afforded criminal justice will be a compelling argument. But no less compelling will be arguments citing the potential police-state dangers of widespread uncontrolled information surveillance of individuals.

This threat may become even more dangerous, since the surveillance of an automated information system can itself be automated, permitting an agency to keep tabs on large numbers of individuals efficiently. Ultimately, the information technology would permit both the tools and the opportunity for widespread surveillance of most of society. At present, the sizable amount of manpower needed to physically observe a person over a period of time acts as a check on such large-scale surveillance.

Finally, there may be a point beyond which a collection of comprehensive information about an individual, although comprised completely of information in the public domain, may assume the characteristics of private information. An individual's concept of private v. public information depends in part on the perception of its completeness and the ways it could be used against him/her.

Other Constitutional Issues

This study has identified several ways in which information systems are posing challenges to interpretations of the fifth, sixth, and by extension to States, the 14th amendments. (See beginning of this chapter for descriptions of these amendments.)

Managerial Due Process

More and more individuals are receiving an increased number of benefits and services from the Government. Information systems have become an indispensable tool for dealing with this growing workload (see ch. 8). To the extent that access to these services in a timely and fair way is a constitutional "due process" concern, the effect of information systems will be to increase scrutiny by the courts and by Congress of the "fairness" of the very large bureaucratic systems that will become established in order to operate service programs.[3]

The following questions about an administrative information system are likely to be of particular interest.

- Whether the information system provides for making timely decisions. While information technology can potentially speed bureaucratic processes, their implementation can often have the opposite effect.[4]
- Whether the information in the system is accurate and timely enough to ensure "fair" decisions. This question is similar to that of "reasonable cause" raised in the criminal justice discussion above.
- Whether there are subtle biases "built in" to the automated system that are invisible to the system operators and agency administrators because they are embedded in the code of the computer. Very large systems that "mass produce" decisions in such areas as health

[3] J. L. Mashaw, "The Management Side of Due Process," *Cornell Law Review*, June 1974, pp. 772-824.

[4] "DC Youth CETA Jobs Program Still Plagued by Delays in Pay," *Washington Post*, July 27, 1980, sec. 8, p. 1, col. 1.

benefits, student loans, or tax returns may react quickly to what the computer recognizes as "normal" applications, but reject "unusual" claims. If, as a consequence, clients are subjected to an unacceptable amount of hassle and delay, the definition of "normal" used by the computer may become subject to due process challenge.

Information Collection

The increased recordkeeping and data collection requirements imposed by the Government on organizations and individuals was one of the trends identified in this study. The quantity of information that individuals and organizations now must provide to the Government—either mandatorily (e.g., for census, tax, or regulatory purposes), in order to receive benefits (e.g., loan guarantees or medical payments), or to justify management decisions—is already extensive and growing larger.

There may be a threat to fifth amendment protections stemming from the use of personal or corporate computer data that have been collected by the Government for one purpose as evidentiary material in unrelated criminal or regulatory cases.

Social/Psychology-Based Applications

In addition to the straightforward uses of information systems to collect data and automate decisions, there are a number of new computer applications that use analytical techniques being developed in social psychology. The actual effectiveness of these techniques, which purport to predict and analyze human behavior based on the statistical analysis of information about individuals, is still being debated. Social scientists anticipate a steady improvement in the ability to predict future social behavior based on the analysis of seemingly unrelated personal characteristics or of the results from batteries of tests. If these capabilities improve as expected, some serious due process questions could be raised by their use in the criminal justice system. Three particular applications already appear to pose problems.

1. *Jury selection:* A small industry has grown up around the use of computerized dossiers of potential jurors along with computer models for predicting juror behavior. At this time, the technology is very expensive and its value is controversial. While some defense lawyers have claimed success owing in part to the use of these systems, it is hard to prove conclusively that the outcome of a particular trial was in any way due to specific juror selection.

   However, future computer technology will make this application cheap, and far more personal data about potential jurors will be available, legally or illegally. Furthermore, there is a sufficiently sound social scientific basis underlying this type of use to suggest that predictive techniques will be likely to improve in effectiveness. If so, the entire concept of an "impartial" jury as required by the sixth amendment may be challenged.[5]
2. *Lie detectors:* Lie detecting technology has already raised many difficult problems for Congress and the courts. Computer-based technology will add a new dimension to these still unresolved issues. So called "voice stress" analyzers are being manufactured and marketed for relatively low prices. This type of lie detector, which analyzes the degree of stress in a speaker's voice, depends on the assumption that measurable stress indicators appear when a lie is being told.

   Unlike older lie detector technology based on the polygraph, voice stress devices can be used without the cooperation or even knowledge of the sub-

[5] John L. Wanamaker, "Computer and Scientific Jury Selection: A Calculated Risk," *University of Detroit Journal of Urban Law,* vol. 55, winter 1978, pp. 345-370.

ject. This single difference puts the use of lie detectors into an entirely new realm of fifth amendment problems, as well as opening up more generally new problems of social interaction in such areas as employer-employee relationships.

There are three distinct problems to be addressed: the effectiveness of such technology, the ways in which it is used by Government agencies and by police, and its use by employers, reporters and others for whom it would be both a tool for their work and a possible means of abusing individual rights to privacy.

3. *Predicting criminal behavior:* Much research has been done on the application of computer-based social science and statistical models to files of personal data and the results of psychological tests, in order to predict behavior. Techniques are being studied for detecting tendencies toward juvenile delinquency, drunken driving, or violent antisocial behavior, and for security checks by the Government. Conceivably, such research could be applicable not only to criminal justice problems, but also to such tasks as approving credit, determining insurability, or hiring and promoting employees.

As social scientists improve this predictive capability, important questions of fifth and 14th amendment rights will be raised. Essentially, individuals may be denied rights, privileges, and benefits based, not on past performance, but on a prediction of future tendencies. Courts will be examining these predictive models very carefully for their accuracy, relevance, and fairness. They will also be addressing the fundamental question of the appropriateness of these models and their potential for discrimination.

The problem will be to establish proper boundaries. Important decisions have often been based on estimates of an individual's future performance. An employee who does well in one job might be expected to perform equally well when promoted. On the other hand, society cannot imprison a person who a computer model predicts may someday rob a bank. But should that knowledge be "reasonable cause" to monitor such a person closely or deny employment?

New information system applications will increase the emphasis on drawing clear boundaries between what ways of using them are and are not acceptable. Particularly difficult equity issues will be raised if the results of such predictive models were to discriminate among groups that have experienced discrimination historically.

Chapter 12

Regulatory and Other Issues

Contents

TABLE

Chapter 12
Regulatory and Other Issues

Regulatory Boundaries

As computer-based information systems evolve, they challenge traditional concepts of boundaries—physical or social—that are reflected in the law and regulatory policy. The integration of computer and communication technologies form systems that cross boundaries between nations, States, and organizations. The issue of transborder data flow discussed below exemplifies the kinds of international problems created by such integration. Others include the following:

- *Interstate conflict:* When States have conflicting laws involving information or information processing, for example, property tax laws that cover computer data bases, an integrated data system that exists in a number of different States can raise difficult questions of legal jurisdiction.

  Furthermore, some States may become data havens because they have weaker laws.* Computer networks also allow State-regulated services such as banking to be offered across State borders, thus challenging traditional attitudes toward single State banking. Telephone bill payer accounts, for example, can be used across State boundaries.
- *Federalism:* Linking Federal data systems with local systems complicates jurisdictional problems even further. The Federal Bureau of Investigation's National Crime Information Center (NCIC) is an example where the traditional autonomy of local and State criminal justice organizations has complicated the Federalism issue (see the OTA assessment of NCIC/CCH, in progress). Similar problems could also arise by linking together Federal and State systems that contain data concerning such matters as taxation, welfare, education, medical care, and drug abuse.
- *Antitrust:* The economics of large integrated data systems, coupled with the potential for increased convenience to the customer, may push service providers to use shared facilities for banking, transportation scheduling, reservation systems, and so on. The Department of Justice and other regulators will be interested in whether such shared facilities create monopolistic barriers to new entrants or are mechanisms for control of the market, or whether they encourage competition by reducing the cost of access for smaller firms.

Information technology is changing form so fast that it is tending to outstrip the working definitions of devices and services that serve as the basis for law and regulation. These definitional problems relate both to the technology itself, and to the products and services that depend on it.

- *Computers or communication:* The best known example is the continuing attempt by the Federal Communications Commission to establish what services and what technologies are already "communications," thus regulated, and what are "computer" services and technologies, thus not regulatable. Their second inquiry on these questions, which began in 1976, only recently resulted in an opinion[1] that is now under

*A system operator could maintain the computer and data base in a State with a lenient legal environment, and access it by a terminal in a State with stricter laws.

[1]Second Computer Inquiry Docket No. 20828, final decision adopted Apr. 7, 1980, FCC 80-189, and reported as 77 FCC 2d 384 (1980). See also the Memorandum Opinion and Order, adopted Oct. 28, 1980, FCC 80-628.

court challenge. Even if the definition is accepted, there is no reason to believe that the problem has been permanently resolved. The general trend toward deregulation of all technology and services, however, may render the question less critical.

- *Branch banking:* Many States have laws that either prohibit or tightly regulate branch banks. An issue that has been debated considerably is whether the automated extensions of banking (e.g. automatic teller machines (ATMs) or pay-by-phone services) constitute "branches" in the usual meaning of the law. Since ATMs and telephone service can be dispersed widely as well as cross borders, significant issues centering on antitrust and interstate banking rest on the way in which a branch is defined (see the OTA assessment of electronic funds transfers, in progress).
- *The status of electronic mail:* Electronic data transmission has opened a major policy question about the definition of mail. As with the computer/communication issue above, this definition is significant because it places a class of services under one or another set of regulations. Unlike many other countries that have combined postal and telecommunication services under one national agency, the United States has pursued completely different approaches to regulating each service category. Electronic mail, in its various forms, provides a new service with features of both manual delivery and telecommunication, and may pose new and difficult regulatory questions (see the OTA assessment of the role of the Postal Service in electronic mail, in progress).
- *Bank information services:* Some very large banks have developed elaborate data processing hardware and software to support their operations. They have found that the sale of these products and information services to other smaller banks can be a profitable enterprise. In their view, it is a natural extension of their banking services. The service bureau industry, which sells access to computers and programs, does not agree. It contends that banks are using their enormous capital resources to enter an entirely new, unrelated field, and should not be allowed to do so under laws that strictly regulate the proper activities of banks.[2] The outcome may hinge on whether these new information services constitute banking in a sense compatible with law.

[2]"Citibank: A Rising Giant in Computer Services," *Business Week*, Aug. 4, 1980, pp. 54-56.

Computer Crime

The changing nature of crime in our information society creates problems in detecting and prosecuting crimes against information systems.[3]

- New types of abuses occur for which there are no appropriate laws.
- Traditional definitions, for instance of theft, may be inapplicable when information is the object of the criminal activity.
- Procuring evidence in information crimes can complicate or stop prosecution.

It may be that these problems will be temporary, and that the legal system will shortly be able to accommodate itself to these types of crimes. It has been suggested,

[3]Susan H. Nycum, *The Criminal Law Aspects of Computer Abuse: Federal Criminal Code* and *The Criminal Law Aspects of Computer Abuse: State Penal Laws*, Stanford Research Institute, 1976.

however, that the inherent nature of information and computer crimes mandates new laws.

Congress has recently considered two bills that address computer crime. The Senate bill would make it a Federal crime to use computers as tools for criminal assault or as its object.* The House** addressed the problem of protecting the providers of in-house information services, in particular cable and broadcast entertainment companies such as Home Box Office, from what is called "pirating."***[4] The information industry feels that unless governmental sanctions are used to protect its products and services, there will be little incentive to provide them. The radio hobbyists, who are among the major "pirates," counter that to date practically no technological safeguards are used by off-the-air pay TV and cable TV, and that reasonable use of more secure technology would safeguard these signals without having to legislate a new class of criminals into existence.

Although neither bill was passed by the 96th Congress, the problems that motivated them remain. It is likely that similar legislation will be introduced in the 97th Congress. Computer crime laws have already been passed by 10 States, and at least another 5 have bills pending[5] (see table 8).

With the support of the Federal Government, researchers are exploring the nature of computer crime, the methods used and the types and motives of criminals.[6] Even without new laws it is of particular importance to inform the staffs of Federal and local law enforcement and criminal justice agencies about the impact of this new type of criminal activity on their work.[7]

Table 8.—States Passing or Considering Computer Crime Legislation

	Passed
Arizona	October 1978
California	January 1980
Colorado	July 1979
Florida	August 1978
Hawaii	(a)
Illinois	September 1979
Massachusetts	(a)
Michigan	March 1980
Missouri	(a)
New Mexico	April 1979
North Carolina	June 1980
Pennsylvania	(a)
Rhode Island	(a)
Utah	May 1979

[a]Legislation Pending.

SOURCE: Computer Business Equipment Manufacturers Association, *State Legislation Status Report, 1980.*

To date, studies of computer crime and computer abuse have emphasized the acts of an individual or group of individuals against an organization. Some observers have noted, however, that the computer can also be used by organizations to take advantage of customers or clients.[8] Customers of organizations using electronic billing, funds transfer, or calculating aids (e.g., supermarket scanners) may simply be defrauded. Furthermore, computer systems are used for making many decisions that affect people's lives, from political apportionment to setting pollution standards and assessing the effectiveness and hazards of a new drug. Therefore, there will likely be some temptation for various interests to misuse the systems they run, for their own purposes.

*S. 240.

**H.R. 7747 (H.R. 6192).

***Pirating is stealing the signal and decoding it, and is easy to do with current technology.

[4]"The Piracy Danger to Subscription TV," *Business Week,* Sept. 29, 1980, pp. 44.

[5]Computer and Business Equipment Manufacturing Association, "First State Legislation Status Report," Washington, D.C., 1980.

[6]Donn B. Parker, *Crime by Computer,* Charles Scribner's Series, New York, 1976.

[7]Department of Justice, *Computer Crime: Criminal Justice Resource Manual,* 1979.

[8]Rob Kling, "Computer Abuse and Computer Crime as Organizational Activities," *Computers and Law Journal,* spring 1980, pp. 403-427.

Transborder Data Flow

During the past several years, international attention has been focused on a collection of issues referred to as transborder data flow. These diverse issues have a common origin in the increased communication of data across national boundaries.[9] In the developed world, they have crystallized around the proliferation of national privacy laws that usually specify the treatment of personal data in domestic systems, and also set standards for the transfer of such data across national boundaries.[10] Several potential problems have emerged that would act to constrain the international flow of information.

- Different and conflicting laws could make the operation of distributed computer systems by large multinational corporations difficult if not impossible.
- Third-party organizations providing computer services across national borders could be inhibited from competing with similar firms operating within countries.
- The extension of privacy protection to the concept of legal persons such as corporations could vastly expand the types of information controlled, by restrictions placed on transmission over national boundaries.

Some efforts are underway to reconcile these various constraints. The Ministers of the Council of Europe have approved model legislation that would provide guidelines for national privacy laws.[11] However, the United States is not a member of the Council, and even more significantly, the U.S. approach to privacy law does not fit the Council model. Thus, from the U.S. perspective the Council approach does not provide a solution.

The Organization for Economic Cooperation and Development has developed a voluntary agreement for its member states that would be more flexible.[12] The initial enthusiasm for a third approach—an international treaty on information flow—appears to have been dampened by the difficulties in getting even a general voluntary agreement.

In general, the U.S. position on this issue has been to favor the free flow of information across borders, and to view the European privacy efforts as principally a disguise for protectionist control of international commercial data processing. Some Europeans maintain that their actions derive principally from their deep concerns about privacy, pointing to historical abuse by totalitarian nations of government and private record systems.[13]

Another aspect of the transborder data flow issue is the concern by the Third World countries that control over information and information flow is a form of international power exerted by the Western nations. This attitude was manifested both in negotiations at the World Administrative Radio Conference[14] and in proposals in the United Nations Educational, Scientific, and Cultural Organization (UNESCO) for a "New Information Order."

[9] R. Turn (ed.), *Transborder Data Flows*, report of the American Federation of Information Processing Societies, Panel on Transborder Data Flow, 1979.

[10] Department of Commerce, *Selected Foreign National Data Protection Laws and Bills*, Office of Telecommunication, special publication 78-19, 1978.

[11] Council of Ministers of the Council of Europe, "Council of Europe Convention for the Protection of Individuals With Regard to Automatic Processing of Personal Data," approved September 1980.

[12] Council of the Organization for Economic Cooperation and Development, *Recommendation of the Council Concerning Guidelines Governing the Protection of Privacy and Transborder Flows of Personal Data*, adopted Sept. 23, 1980.

[13] Department of State, Bureau of Oceans and International Environment and Scientific Affairs, *Selected Papers on International Policy Implications of Computers and Advanced Telecommunications Systems*, January 1979.

[14] See U.S. Congress, Office of Technology Assessment, *Assessment of Radio Frequency Use and Management Impacts From the World Administrative Radio Conference of 1979*, in progress.

The concerns that have been expressed are not just focused on computer systems. They also cover such topics as international news-gathering, access to satellite communication, the spilling of broadcasts over borders, and the exchange of scientific data. However, the fundamental attitudes and goals of the various nations as expressed in their negotiations over international information policy will undoubtedly shape the laws and regulations under which international data systems will be operated in the future.

Information Gap

Some observers have suggested that the advent of information technology will widen the gulf between the haves and the have-nots in society. This view is based on relative differences in what might be called "information literacy," the ability to use information technology to cope with everyday life.

The technology itself is potentially highly flexible. Information systems can be designed to make the use of devices and services far easier than before, for example by providing access to people with language problems and physical handicaps. Research and development (R&D) in such subjects as computer speech, speech understanding, and pictorial display will continue to improve the potential accessibility of information technology.

Whether these capabilities will be used by a system designer is a different question. Making a computer system accessible often imposes added costs for hardware or for more computation. Therefore a concern for efficiency or economy, or the system designer's biases or ignorance, can result in an information system with unequal accessibility built into it.[16]

Should such an information gap develop, it could affect the citizenry in areas such as:

- *Employment:* As automation penetrates the workplace—both manufacturing and white-collar—unemployment may result not so much from increased productivity as from the inability of existing employees to adapt to the new technology. If projections about an evolving information society and economy are correct (see ch. 5), information literacy could become an essential requirement for entering the labor market.
- *Relation with Government:* To the extent that information technology stands between the citizen and a governmental obligation or service, a potential barrier exists. Banks carried out extensive studies with regard to consumer acceptance before undertaking the design of ATM devices. Government agencies, on the other hand, because they do not have the same economic motivation, may not necessarily be very concerned about the acceptability of their systems. (Incentives to have such concern may need to be imposed by law, regulation, or executive policy.) Individuals who are technologically illiterate may be affected in several ways:
  —they may not exercise basic rights such as voting;
  —they may be at a serious disadvantage in legal proceedings, both criminal and civil; and
  —they may find access to such needed services as welfare, health care, and educational benefits, barred or severely impeded.

To the extent that information illiteracy is unevenly distributed among cultural or eco-

[15]Milton R. Wessel, *Freedom's Edge: The Computer Threat to Society* (Reading, Mass.: Addison-Wesley Publishing Co., 1974).

[16]T. Sterling, et al, "Humanizing Information Systems: A Report From Stanley House," *Communications of the Association for Computing Machinery,* November 1974, pp. 609-612.

nomic groups, the consequences would fall disproportionately on the poor and disadvantaged, in general. The gulf between the haves and the have-nots in society might not only be increased but, due to such barriers as a more limited access to jobs, societal efforts to bridge that gulf would be frustrated.

Computer Software Protection

As discussed in chapter 3 and later in chapter 13, the cost of computer software has become a pacesetting factor in development of new computer applications. Increasingly, computer hardware is being designed to fit the software. With the investment so high, the value of software research and development is even greater and the need for proprietary protection felt even more strongly. At the same time, however, there is a strong need for innovation in software R&D, the sharing of ideas, and breakthroughs among researchers.

Copyright and patent protection are the traditional means for protecting the commercial value of information while providing for public disclosure. But the continuing uncertainty concerning copyright and patent protection for computer software leads many software researchers to use the trade secret approach to protect their time and dollar investment. Private firms doing software R&D generally protect software trade secrets through employee nondisclosure agreements, restricted access measures, and by otherwise keeping the work confidential. This of course makes the sharing of information in the software R&D community quite difficult.

The Copyright Act of 1976 specifies that computer programs are copyrightable as "literary works." But the extent of protection defined under the act and more recent court decisions[17] have left the situation ambiguous. Amendments to the act were introduced and enacted in the 96th Congress as the "Computer Software Copyright Act of 1980."[18] However, the issue of computer software protection appears sufficiently important and unsettled to warrant continued congressional attention.[19]

[17] *Data Cash Systems, Inc.* v. *JS&A Group, Inc.*, U.S.D.C., for Northern Illinois, Sept. 26, 1979.

[18] H.R. 6934, Mar. 26, 1980, enacted as an amendment to H.R. 6933, "Government Patent Policy Act of 1980," Public Law 96-517, Dec. 12, 1980, and based on a recommendation of the National Commission on New Technological Uses of Copyrighted Works, *Final Report*, Washington, D.C., 1979.

[19] See "Court Broadens Rules on Patenting Software," *Science*, vol. 211, Mar. 20, 1981, pp. 1325, ff.

Chapter 13
Trends in Computer Technology

Contents

LIST OF FIGURES

Chapter 13
Trends in Computer Technology

Introduction

Computer technology is advancing rapidly, even explosively. To assess the impacts of information systems, the current state of this technology and where it is heading must be understood. The capability that information technology puts in the hands of the computer user determines the nature of the applications that are developed.

Developmental trends are already shaping the nature of the information-based services that will be provided in the coming decade. New services that make use of the growing integration of telecommunication and information technology are being designed and implemented; and both industry and Government are looking at a wide range of innovative products and services that will be used by the in-home information system of the future.

The nature of the technology as it evolves will also influence the structure of the industry associated with it. Companies that specialized only in components are beginning to market computer systems; companies that sold only general purpose computer systems are beginning to market consumer products that incorporate these systems.

For the purposes of this study, emphasis has been placed on what information systems can do rather than on the fundamental nature of electronic technology. Many interesting developments now in the laboratory, such as Josephson junctions,* may not fundamentally change either the nature of the systems that are designed or the purposes to which they will be put, particularly over the next 10 years. Other developments, such as the microprocessor, are today revolutionizing the ways in which computers are used as well as the thinking about their potential social impacts. Overall, the anticipated changes from laboratory developments over the next several years will be more of degree than of form.

*A Josephson junction is a microscopic-size electronic logic device that operates at the temperature of liquid helium. It is very fast and uses very little power.

Conclusions

Several conclusions can be drawn from OTA's analysis of the trends in the development of computer technology over the next 10 or 15 years. Spurred by both industrial and Government research and development (R&D) programs, information systems are undergoing a revolution that will be manifested by a proliferation of new products and services affecting all sectors of American society.

Hardware

- Computer electronics are experiencing an extraordinary drop in price, increase in power, and reduction in size.

In 1977, the Privacy Protection Study Commission estimated that the cost of computing would drop by a factor of more than 100 during the 20-year period from 1970 to

1990. This means that the million dollar computer of the 1960's will cost less than a thousand dollars in the late 1980's.

Concomitantly, during this same period calculating speed is expected to increase a hundredfold. In 1970, the largest processors performed 10 million operations per second, today they perform 100 million, and by 1990 there will be a processor that will perform 1 billion. In addition to greater speed, new designs can also greatly increase the power of future computer systems.

The large computer that occupied one or several rooms in the late 1960's will fit in a desk drawer by the late 1990's, and a medium-size computer will fit in a briefcase or even a coat pocket. These trends do not necessarily mean that in all cases the costs of purchasing, programing, and operating a large computer application system will decrease. Rather, more work will be done for the equivalent number of dollars.

- There will be a great expansion in the number of computers being used in business, education, and the home.

This effect is already being seen. The home computer boom, which was the first big stimulus for the computer retailing stores, has fallen off slightly, only to give way to a new marketing thrust aimed at small businesses. The hand calculator, which has become a ubiquitous tool, is already being supplanted. A small hand-held computer is now available in the consumer market, and electronic calculators are being built into wristwatches. Computers are also being used as part of office automation.

- Computers will be used as components in a wide range of consumer products.

With the advent of an integrated circuit microprocessor that will sell in mass quantities for $1 or less, the use of the computer for controlling everyday devices in the home and at work will become commonplace. Computers are already being used or designed to control such devices as clothes washers, sewing machines, home thermostats, automobile engines, sprinkler systems, typewriters, filing systems, electric lights, and cash registers.

While many applications will involve simply substituting electronic for mechanical control, the increased "intelligence" incorporated in the products will be used to provide such additional features as energy conservation or self-diagnosis of errors, and to give more flexible control to the user.

- New products and services based on computer and telecommunication technology will become available.

In addition to adding computer control to familiar products, the new computer technology will be used to provide a new range of products and services for the home and business. The video game and home computer are just the first of a long line of computer-based information products and services that will appear. (Electronic funds transfer and electronic mail, two examples of information services, are examined in separate OTA reports.)

- There will be a continuing, rapid increase in the power of very large computer systems.

Advances in speed, efficiency, and microelectronics coupled with new design concepts will produce computers in the 1980's that are far more powerful than the biggest ones now available. This type of power is useful for a limited but important set of computational applications, e.g., improved systems for weather prediction. Furthermore, systems that manage very large data bases require very powerful computer processors, particularly when sophisticated searches and analyses must be made.

Software

- Software technology is expanding steadily, although not as rapidly as the hardware.

Computer programs are sets of basic instructions that tell the computer the steps to take in doing a task. Programs can contain millions of instructions, and their design is as varied as the number of ways computers are used. While computer scientists have been successful in developing theoretical models of computer hardware logic, efforts to build an equivalent theory of programs have not been rewarding to date. Thus, developing systematic techniques for creating, testing, and monitoring computer software has been a slow and tedious process. Some experts maintain that programing is still more of an art than a science.

The continuing R&D on programing languages and software engineering will provide a flow of improved techniques and software tools, but the rate of improvement will not match the explosive growth in hardware capability.

- New software techniques will allow computers to process a wider variety of data.

Traditionally, computers have processed either numerical or alphabetic data structured in very rigid formats. However, software for processing text, graphic images, and digitized voice is developing rapidly in addition to software for processing data alone. The result will be new families of products and services affecting Government, industry, and the citizen at home.

- Software technology is the limiting factor in controlling the rate at which new applications appear.

The use of the new specialized hardware that is being designed is confined to very restricted purposes, or is merely putting existing software ideas into hardware form for increased efficiency. The software basis for most new computer applications in the 1980's exists now. There does not appear to be much likelihood that a new concept of computer design will change the way computers are used in the next decade. Rather, the changes will be in the scale of their use and in who will be using them.

- The predominant cost of information systems will be for the software; the information industry will become increasingly labor intensive.

This conclusion follows directly from the last two statements coupled with the labor intensive nature of programing. This trend will influence the marketing practices of computer manufacturers, who will increasingly find profit in the sales of complete systems—combinations of hardware and software—rather than hardware by itself.

- Software reliability, security, and auditability will improve slowly.

Large systems, because they are complex and cumbersome, tend to suffer from the kinds of reliability problems that are not solved by building more reliable hardware. The problems of assuring that a system is actually performing as intended and cannot be compromised, accidentally or deliberately, are inherent in the complexity of software design.

Furthermore, although computer software experts are improving their understanding of how to increase the reliability of programs, they are unable to keep pace with the growth in the size and complexity of the systems being designed. Recently, system designers have become more aware of the need to design secure and auditable applications, and users have become aware that they can demand such capabilities from the producers. Thus, although some improvement is taking place, substantial progress will depend on more R&D.

- New data base techniques will allow massive data banks that serve multiple uses.

Data bases will grow; some will contain trillions of units of information. At the same time, people will want to work with the data in more varied ways. Today, sophisticated programing is often required in order to handle efficiently each different type of query a user might want to make of the data base.

However, researchers are developing methods to improve the efficient use of large data bases and to make them serve multiple needs. This is being done through the development of more powerful query languages, new ways of organizing the data within the machine, and new hardware designs.

Human-Computer Interface

People communicate with computers for three basic reasons: to describe the task to be done, to enter data for processing, and to derive results. Improvements in this technology will result not only in less costly systems, but also in a vast expansion of information systems capabilities and in their more efficient use.

- There will be an increase in the direct use of computers by nonexperts.

Improvements in programing languages will allow users to communicate more easily with the computer. Historically, programing and system control languages have been complicated and time-consuming to learn. They often require understanding how a computer operates. New, easy-to-learn but powerful languages will increase the number of people who will use computers directly without recourse to an intermediary expert. In addition, the proliferation of computer introductory courses in high schools will increase the number of people who have a basic knowledge of computer systems.

This trend will allow many more simple applications to be developed by users individually or in modest organizational settings. However, in larger organizations, or for applications that require integration with other systems, it will mean that much of the programing for modern small systems will be done by end users in industry and in the home who are not subject to control by central data processing management. This may lead to such problems as misuse, poorly functioning systems, or incompatibility.

- More data will be captured by computers and stored in machine-readable form.

The distribution of computing power through the use of microprocessors linked together over communication lines will increase the amount of data captured at the source and stored in computer-readable form. Some types of information are captured deliberately, as in the case of the computerized register in a retail store. Other types, which are captured only as a byproduct of automation, may be found to be useful enough to keep. For example, the system data collected by word processing systems may be considered useful by managers in monitoring secretarial efficiency. The proliferation of capturing such data may raise serious policy issues.

- Output will be organized to present information that is more directly useful to the user.

It has been known from the earliest days of computing that the form in which the results of computations are presented can determine, in great part, whether it is actually used or whether the answer being sought is found. Advances in both the hardware and programing for image display and speech are being brought out of the laboratory and into the commercial market.

Research in information display is discovering how to filter significant information from insignificant data and present it to the user in the most efficient way. There is now a new, burgeoning interest in the use of color graphics display, a technology long considered the domain of the computer research laboratory, but too expensive for general use.

- There will be increased interface with information systems by consumers in their homes and employees in their offices.

Many systems designed for entertainment, education, information retrieval, and computational services are beginning to be offered through a combination of evolving television sets and telephone instruments because of easy-to-use software, data banks, and the distribution medium provided by cable television (CATV). As a result, there is a possibility that society as a whole will be substantially affected, but to what extent is presently unknown.

Communication

The rapidly increasing availability of inexpensive digital data communication through specialized networks such as Telenet and Tymnet, coupled with the trend of manufacturers to design systems with elaborate communication hardware and software built in, are motivating growth in the use of distributed, communication-based systems. New satellite-based data communication services will further stimulate this trend.

- The use of distributed data bases and distributed processing will grow rapidly.

Rather than centralizing data collection and processing as in the past, the most efficient procedure in the future will be to localize these functions at the point where the data are originally captured. Organizations will have computational capacity distributed among all of their offices. All computer-based devices, even word processors, will be linked into the central system.

The problems in managing such a distributed system will be a major concern of large organizations. In particular, procedures for controlling access and for ensuring data quality will be more difficult in a distributed environment. However, dealing with them effectively will be crucial to the successful operation of communication-based systems.

- There will be increased availability of computer services to the home and business over communication lines.

Many homes will have small computers or computer terminals, and those that do not will likely contain telephones and television sets that have been equipped with computer control. All of these devices will provide links from the home and office to a multitude of information services provided over a variety of communication channels such as television broadcast, telephone, or cable lines.

Processors

The 1970's have seen continual dramatic improvements in the characteristics of the components from which computers are made. It is expected that this trend will continue through the 1980's, with computing hardware becoming remarkably inexpensive and efficient.

The decline in cost per logic function from 1960 projected to 1990 is shown in figure 8. In 1960, the price of a logic gate ranged from $1 to $10 per unit, depending on speed. By 1990, that price is expected to range from a few thousandths of a cent to a few tenths of a cent per gate. This continuing decline is based in large part on the dramatic increase in capability of semiconductor chips, as illustrated in figure 9.

There has been a parallel increase in the speed of processing. In 1960, the fastest machine executed about 1 million instructions per second. By 1990, there probably will be computers that will execute a billion or more instructions per second, a thousandfold increase in speed.

This combination of increased speed and decreased cost for logic components results in a steady decline in the cost of computation. The drop in the costs of computing on IBM systems that are roughly equivalent, over the period 1952 through 1980, is shown in figure 10.

These gains have all been due to progress in integrated circuit technology, the process by which electronic components are printed on small chips of silicon. Using these chips as components has resulted in a steady shrinkage of the size of computers from assemblages that filled several rooms to the current desk-top versions. Mass production techniques have replaced the hand-wiring of

Figure 8.—Projections of Logic Cost per Gate

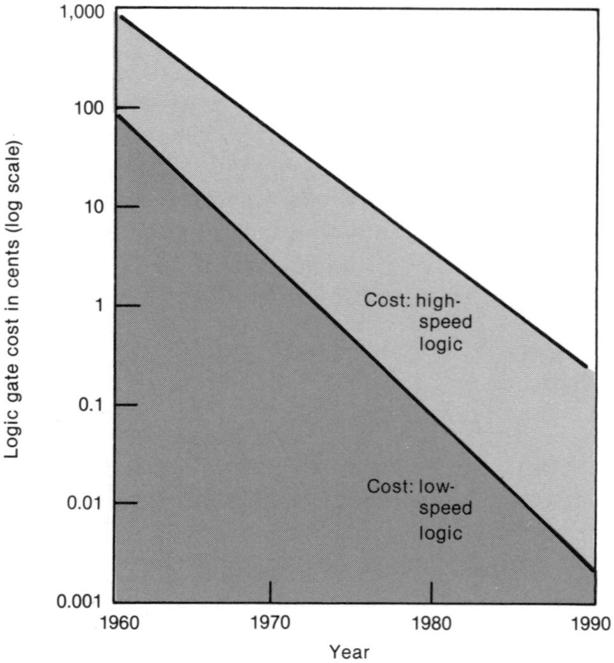

SOURCE: Office of Technology Assessment and Privacy Protection Study Commission.

Figure 9.—Increase in Capability of Semiconductor Chips From 1956 to 1980

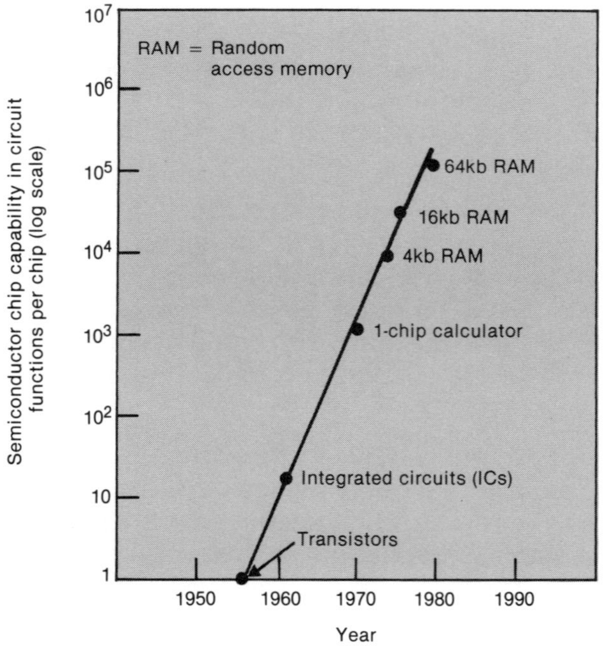

SOURCE: Institute of Electrical and Electronic Engineers, *IEEE Spectrum*, vol. 17, June 1980, p. 48. U.S. Manufactures of semiconductor chips include firms such as Intel, Motorola, Texas Instruments, Rockwell, National Semiconductor, and Zilog.

Figure 10.—Drop in Average Computer System Cost per 100,000 Calculations From 1952 to 1980

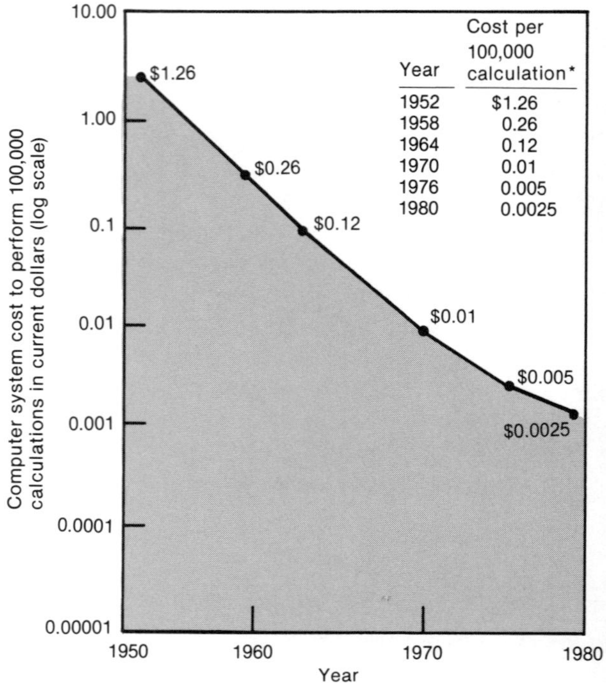

*Cost per 100,000 calculation is based on data for the following IBM computer systems (with year in parentheses): 701 (1952), 7090 (1058), 360/50 (1964), 370/168 (1970), 3033 (1976), 4300 (1980).

SOURCE: Office of Technology Assessment and President's Reorganization Project, *Federal Data Processing Reorganization Study: Basic Report of the Science and Technology Team,* Washington, D.C., June 1978, pp. 29-30.

a decade ago, speeding up the manufacturing phase. Energy consumption, both to operate the computer system directly and for the necessary system cooling, has dropped enormously.

The financial implications of these latter trends are significant in that they are stimulating a rapid growth in computer applications that will accelerate beyond their current high rate in the 1980's. Facility costs have historically been a major expense to users installing computers. Now, many systems take up only a desk top, require no specialized environment control, and plug into a normal electrical wall socket. This flexibility means that many computer systems can be installed at any site, from the home to the business, with little or no added cost for preparing the physical site.

Inexpensive very large-scale integration (VLSI) based computer hardware will also lead to lower maintenance costs in the 1980's. Maintenance currently is estimated to cost about 5 percent of the computer's purchase price per year for medium-size computers. The figure is higher for smaller machines. A reduction in these costs will result from lower failure rates, easier maintenance by replacing larger modular units of the system, and built-in hardware redundancy and fault diagnosis.

Implications: These trends have several implications for computer hardware. In the first place, as illustrated in figure 10, there has been and will continue to be a steady drop in the cost of computing on general purpose, medium- to large-scale computing systems.

Second, small inexpensive, personal desktop computers have appeared on the market in the last few years. These "microcomputers," while modest by present standards, are quite powerful relative to the standards of only a decade or two ago. The price of these systems will drop rapidly, and their capacity will grow over the next decade. These small systems will likely drive the development of a true mass market for computers, a market analogous to the current one for hand calculators.

In addition to making the microcomputer possible, the ability to mass-produce chips and to custom design them at the same time, using the automated production machines, means that there will be a proliferation of special-purpose computers that are custom-made for specific applications. One of the motivations for the development of the so-called "general purpose" computer was that a computer system was expensive and difficult to design and build. Thus, many different user markets had to be identified for a single design in order to provide a sufficient customer base to justify its production.

This view of the manufacturers was reproduced in miniature within each computer center, which accumulated as many different types of applications as possible in order to justify acquiring a large computing machine, and thereby benefit from economies of scale.

These days, however, it is feasible to build special-purpose machines, because the specialized markets have grown and because the cost of designing and marketing custom tailored systems has dropped. As an example, a variety of firms (some quite small) are marketing so-called "array processors," computers designed to calculate the solutions to systems of mathematical equations that display certain special characteristics. These processors are designed to be connected to a general purpose computer, and to be called on only for the specific calculations at which they excel. In the jobs for which they are intended, these array processors, which cost about as much as a large computer, are hundreds of times more powerful than the biggest computers available. The market for this machine exemplifies the increasing ability of small firms to enter the computer hardware business and carve out a niche for themselves.

Basic R&D in hardware design is picking up again after a hiatus. It moved out of the academic and pure research laboratory in the 1960's due to the high costs of building hardware and the lack of enthusiasm for new design concepts on the part of manufacturers. Now, the costs and feasibility of experimental research have improved dramatically. The result should be a proliferation in the 1980's of small specialized computers, tailored to particular needs. This trend will reduce computing costs even more than would result from the drop in component costs alone.

In general, experts expect that a continuing trend will be seen toward modular computer architecture. Logical functions will be distributed over the entire system. The central processor will be a traffic director controlling the flow of work among the various units. There will be specialized computation units like the array processor discussed above, file management processors for handling data bases, communications control units, specialized language processors, and others. Because of widespread high-speed digital communications, these various components will not need to be in the same room or even the same city to be part of the system.

Information Storage

A computer memory comes in a wide variety of sizes, speeds, and types. Any particular system uses an assortment of memories to support its operation. Its most significant design characteristics are *retrieval time* and *capacity.*

Retrieval time is the time it takes to get a segment of information from the memory. The technology currently available provides a range of times from 1 nanosecond (1 billionth of a second) to a minute or more. Retrieval time includes the time both to find and to read the information.

Capacity is the amount of information that can be stored conveniently and economically. It is measured in *bits* (the smallest fundamental unit of information), or *bytes,* an 8-bit grouping roughly equivalent in information content to a single alphabetic character or two numerical digits.

There is a distinct tradeoff between speed and capacity. Therefore, in connecting a computer that performs millions of instructions in a second with a world that operates in a much slower timeframe, a hierarchy of memory types is used. The current selection of memory technology available to system designers is shown in figure 11, and the projected drop in cost for information storage through 1990 is shown in figure 12.

Figure 11.—Cost and Access Time of Memory Technologies

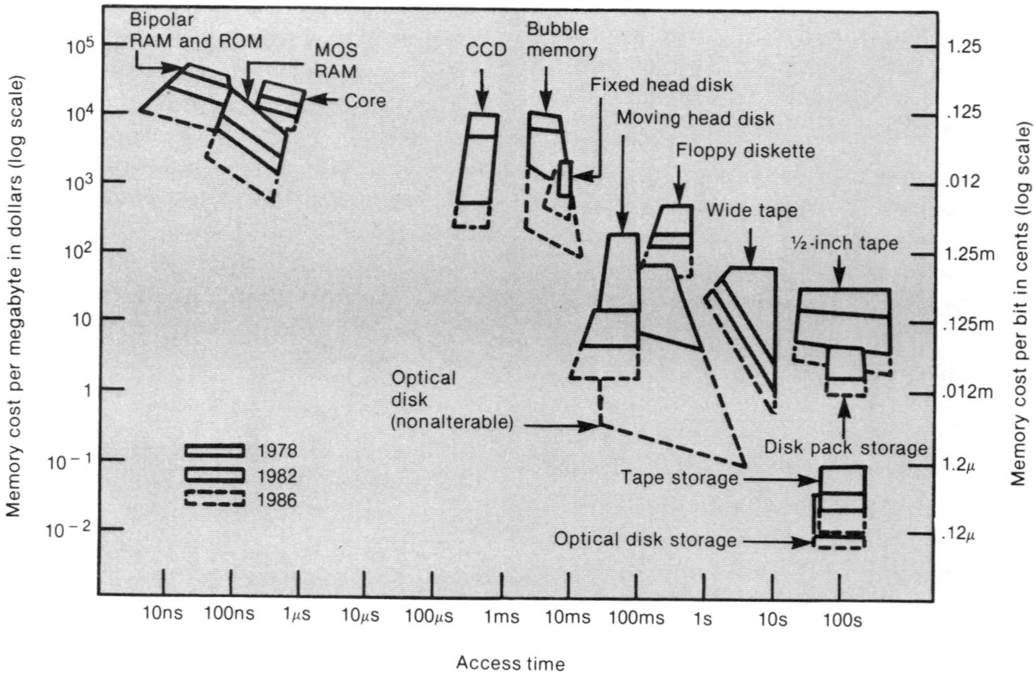

SOURCE: Institute of Electrical and Electronic Engineers. *IEEE Spectrum*, vol. 18, March 1981, p. 41.

Figure 12.—Projections for Memory Cost per Character

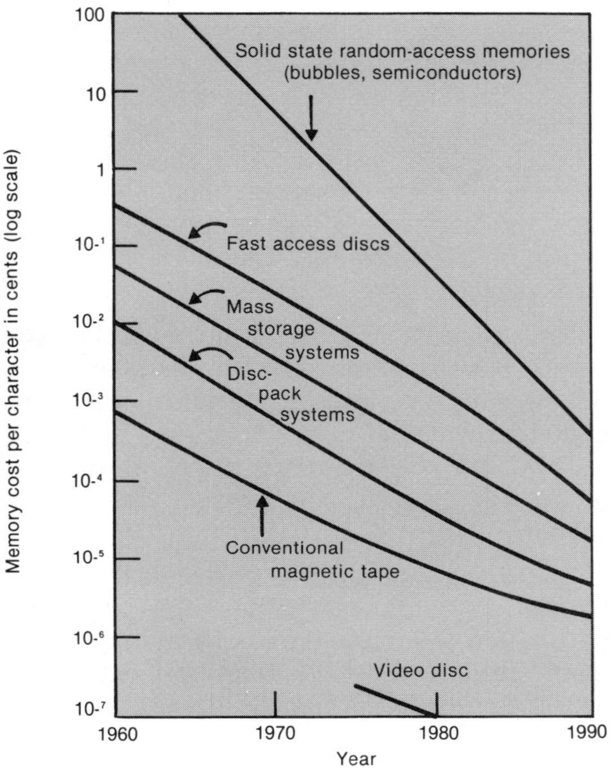

SOURCE: Office of Technology Assessment and Privacy Protection Study Commission.

There are two other important characteristics of various memory systems that affect their use in particular applications. These are *volatility* and *writability.*

Volatility refers to the long-term stability of the memory. Many storage systems lose the information they contain when the power source is removed or interrupted. Others keep the information indefinitely until it is changed.

Writability refers to the ability to insert information in the memory. Memory is classified as read/write or read only, depending on whether or not the computer can copy new data back into the storage in about the same time scale as information can be read. Read only memories are written once and the recording is permanent. In this discussion, memory is roughly categorized as *fast, intermediate,* and *mass storage.*

Fast Memory Storage

Fast memory storage constitutes the upper left-hand group in figure 11. It is the most closely connected to the processor, and hence its speed must be consistent with that of the computer hardware. Because of the relatively high cost of fast memory, it is usually the smallest memory in the system.

For many years, core memories based on the magnetic properties of an iron compound were the principal technology used for fast memory storage. However, this technology seems to have reached its limit in cost, speed, and size. Most new memories now are designed around VLSI semiconductor technology.

Intermediate Memory Storage

Intermediate memory storage, which is reasonably fast but inexpensive enough to be used in large quantities, serves as a buffer between the high-speed semiconductor memory and the very slow mass storage devices. In the long term, *bubble memory* may develop into the technology of choice for intermediate memory storage. Information is stored as tiny magnetic domains that circulate along a printed track in a semiconductor medium. Some bubble memory products are already on the market, and new improved ones are being announced continually.

One of the advantages of bubble memories is that the domains are stable. Therefore, when a bubble memory is used in a terminal, for example, data can be entered and stored in it for later transmission without needing to keep the terminal hooked up continuously to a power supply. The technology of bubble memories is progressing rapidly. One manufacturer has already announced plans to market a million-bit chip that will cost around $2,000 in small quantities.

High-speed magnetic disks are still widely used for intermediate memory, and will continue to be the most important technology for this decade. Steady improvements will be announced throughout the 1980's. Some experts predict that disks will eventually be used in a more finely stratified memory hierarchy, rather than being replaced by bubble memories. This may depend on whether progress in expanding the capacity of bubble memories continues as rapidly as it has.

Mass Memory Storage

Progress seems to be slower in the area of very large storage devices. No radically new technology has appeared that seems to promise any breakthroughs. Magnetic tape will continue to be used heavily over the next decade.

Many new mass storage technologies—e.g., video disk—are difficult and expensive to write, but very cheap and easy to reproduce and read. Erasing and rewriting are often impossible. Costs per bit of storage for archival applications are low enough to be competitive with paper storage. Incremental improvements over the next decade should strengthen this advantage and stimulate a trend toward permanent document storage in electronic form.

Inexpensive Mass Storage

The rising market for small inexpensive computer systems is producing a demand for small, very cheap, bulk storage technology. The technology is different from that provided for large systems. The size of bulk storage needed is less, and there is more tolerance for slow search times. Currently, personal computers are supported by two types of bulk storage, magnetic tape cassettes and "floppy" disks.

Tape readers are very cheap, as is the tape itself. However, read time is quite slow, even by personal computer standards. Floppy disk hardware is more expensive, although still within the requisite price range. The disks themselves are cheap and easily stored.

Some manufacturers, particularly those marketing computer games, sell programs permanently written on solid-state read only memories (ROM). While relatively expensive as a medium, ROM has the advantage of being difficult to copy, thus discouraging the pirating of software. The ROM approach has not been well accepted by the marketplace, however.

Software

Computer software is also a form of technology. Although it is not a tangible product like a piece of hardware, software shares many of the same characteristics. Much R&D carried out by computer scientists concern software problems. It often results in new concepts and basic techniques for organizing data and sequencing instructions to enable a computer to accomplish a particular task.

Very large programs are harder to analyze, design, and produce than are equally large machines that run them. Consequently, the state-of-the-art in software lags behind that of hardware.

Occasionally, a major breakthrough in programing can motivate new machine designs. For example, a wave of new small processors has appeared on the market to support signal processing applications. These processors are based on the "fast Fourier transform" algorithm, an important discovery made a few years ago that allowed the solutions to certain types of mathematical computations to be calculated 10 times faster than previously.* Even greater speeds

*The Fourier transform itself is a pre-20th century mathematical technique. The advance was a new way to perform the numerous and tedious computations the technique requires.

have been achieved by using special processors to take advantage of this algorithm.

Limits

One area of research that will affect software development in the 1980's is fundamental research in computational complexity. Until recently, fundamental theory in computer science was concerned with computability—whether a computer could calculate an answer to a problem. However, the class of problems that the computer could theoretically solve was enormous. More recently, researchers have been exploring the more practical questions of how easily a problem may be solved, how fast, and how much computer power would be required. The answers have been surprising. Many categories of problems have been found to be almost impossible to solve, that is, the best program possible on the fastest computer available would take many years, even millions of years, to calculate an answer. Such results have already had practical application. For example, they have led to the development of new types of cryptographic codes with interesting new properties. Future research may lead to the ability to calculate theoretically the breakability of a code.

Over the next decade of ever increasing computer power, some types of problems are likely to remain intractable. Complexity theory will help improve the understanding of these limits of computers as they are now designed. Furthermore, it may possibly motivate some radical new concepts in computer design.

Data Base Systems

There is a trend toward the use of large integrated data base systems that support multiple applications. Researchers have been developing methods for organizing data so that it can be accessed in many ways, not all of which may be predicted when the system is designed. Some of the most general data structures, such as relational data bases, are not as yet efficient for very large data bases, but are appearing in commercial products for use with medium-sized systems. New developments in data handling algorithms, and new hardware designs specifically tailored to the support of data access systems, should provide continually improving capabilities during the 1980's.

Improved query languages will allow the information user to interact directly with the computer to obtain the needed data. The integration of better report generators* with the data base system will allow the output to be produced in a more directly usable form. These advances will provide the system user with access to the data base which is much more direct than is now the case. Currently, the normal practice is to work through an intermediary, both to frame the initial inquiry and to interpret the results.

The capability to transfer information between data bases over communication networks will also be improved. This capability, already well-developed in some specific systems, will allow more general exchange among systems connected to commercial data networks. Standard protocols and forms will be agreed on. True distributed data bases are systems in which the location of any particular item of information in the data base may be anywhere in a national or even international network, and in which access to that data is handled totally by the system. These should start to appear commercially in the 1980's.

The increasing size of data bases, the multiplicity of their uses, the wider remote access to them, and their integration over telecommunication lines will all present problems in preserving the security and integrity of the information. It will be more challenging to protect the privacy of personal data or the security of economically valuable information on such distributed systems.

*Report generators retrieve information needed by a manager, perform moderate calculations on it, and organize it in a readable and usable form.

Languages

Languages are the means by which users describe to the computer the kinds of operations they want performed by the system. *Machine language* is the set of instructions that is wired into the computer. Although some machine language programing is still done, it is very difficult and inefficient to use due to the size and complexity of most applications. Modern systems on a medium-sized computer may contain more than a million machine language instructions.

Faced with these difficulties, programers turn to a *higher level language* to write most software. As computers have grown larger and more complex, and as the tasks demanded of them become more complicated, there has been a continual trend toward the use of languages designed to be more representative of the way humans express problem-solving procedures.

In addition to increasing programing efficiency, developers of higher level languages have other goals. Some special languages are tailored to produce efficient codes for particular classes of applications. Others have been developed based on the perception that programing a computer is a form of mental problem-solving, and that the language as the vehicle for that effort is an intellectual tool that can directly help thought processes. Finally, there has been a trend to develop languages that integrate users more closely with the system, thus lowering the degree of expertise required to program the computer. By programing in these user oriented languages, persons who are not computer specialists can interact directly with a system rather than through a professional programer intermediary.

The rapid expansion in the use of large data base systems that serve many users over communication networks is driving a major development effort in *query languages*. They are the means by which a user gains access to a data base, describes the desired information and specifies the format in which it is to be presented.

A principal driving force toward further language development is economics. Hardware costs are decreasing while labor costs are increasing. Developing languages that will increase the productivity of programers has become a high priority. Ultimately, some researchers envision automatic programing in which users specify the problem to be solved in a language close to that used in their environment—engineering, law, medicine, and so on. The computer, using this problem statement, would write its own program.

Full development of such automatic programing systems is far in the future, although simple systems for preparing management reports and models derived from data bases are already in use. More short-term effort is being concentrated on developing tools that help the programer use the computer as an active agent assisting in the creation of a system.

Progress is expected to be slow. It will be impeded by the sheer difficulty of matching the essential ambiguity of human thought and language with the absolute rigidity of computer language. It is also economically difficult to implement radical new languages that require substantial retraining of programers. Finally, there is a reluctance to write programs in languages that are not widely used and known, for the usefulness of a program so written may be unnecessarily restricted.

Software Engineering

For most of the history of computers, programing has been considered an art rather than a form of controlled design. Emphasis was on the ingenuity and elegance of the product, rather than on more mundane measures of utility. Creativity will always have a place in good programing, but its emphasis conflicts with managerial imperatives for economy, control, and predictability. In particular, when the development of a major system requires the coordination of hundreds of programers writing millions of lines of code, the project must be managed in such a way as to guarantee a usable product, on time, and at a reasonable cost.

The relatively new discipline of software engineering has been attempting the difficult task of developing techniques both for programing and for managing the programing of large software systems. The operating system and support software of a large multiprocessor computer system is extraordinarily complex. However, the economic imperative will force work in this area and assure the quick adoption of new results.

Until the present time, efforts have been geared to developing both techniques for breaking a large proposed system into successively smaller logical subunits that can be assigned to programing teams, and ways in which to manage the work of the programers and the communications among them. These and related techniques will gradually become commonplace over the next 5 to 10 years as they are learned by the next generation of programing professionals and managers.

Input-Output Technology

The principal means of communication with a computer has traditionally been through a form of typed input and alphanumeric printed output. Although this type of communication will continue to dominate in the near future, it is inadequate for many new applications. Advances in technology for human-computer interaction will change the way in which computers are used by many people.

Graphics

Graphical display of information is becoming more economically viable, and the technology, both hardware and software, is improving in its capability. In the last few years, researchers have developed efficient techniques for removing hidden lines in order to display solid objects and for combining half-tone, shaded image production with color. Some current research is focused on developing techniques that model various surface reflectivities and textures with respect to different types of light sources.

While work is proceeding on improving the speed of graphical computations to allow the terminal to display very high resolution pictures fast enough to depict motion, such a capability may remain very expensive over the next few years for any but the most simple types of pictures.

Sharp cost breaks are expected for displays with lower image quality. The use of bit-mapped frame buffers, which store slow computer graphics output and play it back at normal speed over a display terminal, will grow as the costs of memories drop.

Some research is being pursued on holographic output of three-dimensional images. However, holographic display is not expected to become widely used in the next decade.

Computer graphics technology is already finding widespread commercial use for creating animated films. It competes favorably with traditional manual techniques. The uses range from pure and commercial art to the production of educational films. Computer languages and graphics software have been developed to allow artists and designers to interact directly with the computer, generally through the display screen, to create their images.

In computer-aided design, the user is interactively coupled to a display screen with a graphical data base and analytical programs stored on a computer. Designers use the computer and the display to develop their designs on a screen. For example, an architect designing a building on the graphics display can have an instantaneous computation of cost, and a civil engineer can do stress calculations while designing a bridge. Computer-aided design has emerged from its infancy. Steady improvements in software and decreasing computing costs will likely make it the methodology of choice for most engineering design in the 1980's. Even today, integrated circuits and printed circuit boards are preferentially designed by these techniques.

Graphical output of computer data can transmit information that is difficult or even impossible to derive from a printout list of numbers. Whether calculating stresses in an airplane wing, the water flow in a flood plain, or the molecular structure of an enzyme, the numerical output of the computer calculations must be translated into a picture before any sense can be made from the results.

Voice Communication

Voice communication with computers is on the verge of becoming commercially successful. The advances have been both in developing better and cheaper computational techniques for generating and recognizing speech and in learning more about the ways in which such systems could be used. This new understanding has lowered the estimates of what would constitute a commercially useful level of performance. Capabilities far short of a human level of performance can markedly enhance communication between human and computer. Some experts even expect a voice-driven typewriter to be on the market before the end of the decade.

There are two basic problems in speech synthesis—first, creating a voice tone carrying a phoneme (a fundamental linguistic element of speech), and second, stringing these phonemes together to make a sentence or phrase. Although neither problem has been solved to the ultimate point of producing natural human-sounding sentences, the technology is improving rapidly. It has already reached the point of commercial utility.

Several companies sell chips in the $10 range to synthesize speech sounds. Texas Instruments offers a mass-produced electronic toy, Speak and Spell®, to help children learn to spell.

One important application of speech is a reader for use by the blind that converts typed text into spoken words. While currently very expensive, these devices should become more economical in the near future.

Speech recognition is a more difficult problem, since the system must deal with an input having great variability. The voice and style of speech varies widely among individuals; the computer recognizer is potentially confronted by a wider array of potential vocabulary to identify; and it must analyze a multiplicity of grammatical structures. Again, entrepreneurs have found that even the very limited capabilities now possible are marketable.

So-called "continuous speech" recognition, understanding natural speech, is still in the research laboratory. While large-scale commercial systems are not expected in the short term, the strong market already developing for limited range speech recognition systems will motivate R&D and encourage the rapid commercialization of research results as they appear.

The best performance to date in a research laboratory environment has been shown by a system that can recognize sentences 91 percent of the time from multiple speakers using a vocabulary of 1,011 words. Major research efforts are proceeding at IBM and at a few university laboratories. Commercial devices with small vocabularies are now being marketed.

Image Recognition

Image recognition presents another form of the problem of recognizing patterns of data. The state-of-the-art is at a similar point. Simple self-contained patterns not in a confusing context can be recognized. Devices on the market read standard typewriter and even handprinted characters. Point-of-sale scanners in stores read and recognize the universal product code on packages drawn across the unit at various speeds and orientations. However, analyzing a more general picture for a variety of elements is a more complicated task, one which, like speech, may depend upon some "understanding" of the context of the pattern.

Slow but steady advances in pattern recognition technology are occurring. The sharp drop in cost for the requisite technology is increasing the range of potential applications.

Data Communication

The ability to move data quickly over long distances through the use of new digital communication technology has had a significant impact on the design and use of information processing systems. Designers now have the opportunity to build systems with greater power than was previously possible, enhancing their ability to process information and provide it to the user in a timely manner. More importantly, however, telecommunication has brought the user closer to the computer by allowing direct interaction with the processing system. As a result, the use of information processing technology has become an integral part of the day-to-day work of many organizations whose operations have become totally dependent on a computer system.

Only technology that relates directly to the development of computer-based information systems is discussed here. (For a detailed analysis of communication technology, see the OTA assessment report entitled, *An Assessment of Telecommunication Technology and Public Policy*.

Digital Communication Technology

The steady improvement of telecommunication service over the last quarter century has benefited the design of computer systems by decreasing their cost and improving their reliability. Significant applications using communications date back to the early 1960's. However, the cost and complexity of putting together a communication-based computer system restricted its use to applications, such as reservation systems, that had an inherent need for remote data entry and display.

Existing communication carriers and new enterprises are beginning to offer new data communication services. These services are designed to provide inexpensive high-speed communication capacity specifically designed for use by computer systems. With these new services available, a host of new communication-based applications will appear over the next decade.

Traditional communication systems have been tailored to carrying voice. The characteristics of voice communication are quite different from those of data communication between computers or between computers and people. The voice telephone network, through switching, provides a temporary line connecting two users. The charges are based on the length of the line provided and the length of time it is made available.

Data communication tends to come in very high-speed bursts, with long periods of silence between transmissions. To perform this type of communication on a traditional telephone network is inefficient, as the line is unused for most of the time. One approach has been to design a network with multiple path connections. Packets of information, along with a destination address, are sent over any instantaneously available path, and the user is charged for the quantity of information transmitted and for the connection with the network. One payoff in sharing traffic from a larger community to obtain better line usage is lower user costs. Secondary benefits include error-free performance and higher reliability. This type of communication facility is called packet switching, and is available as a commercial service. Thus, a librarian in Washington, D.C., with a terminal can dial a local number to access the Washington entry to a national data communication network. Through that network, the librarian can access a bibliographic data base in Los Angeles, and do so at a low cost.

Digital Communication as Part of the System

Viewed in the context of computer system operations, data communications are no different from any other application. However, they do introduce new capabilities and problems to the design, implementation, and operation of information systems.

Early implementations of the data communication programs were designed to take advantage of processor cycles that could not be used productively by other applications. However, the growth in the communication workload, combined with other new tasks that may have been loaded onto the processor, can saturate it and create a need to move the communication management from the central computer to a peripheral processor.

Fully programable front-end processors support the trend of moving communication processing away from the central computer. In some cases these devices have been specifically designed for communication processing. In other cases, general purpose minicomputers are being used as front ends. Either way, the availability of inexpensive logic and memory components has contributed to the further distribution of the communication function away from the central processor.

Security Capabilities

Computers have handled sensitive data and programs for many years; however, it is only recently that the need to secure them has become a serious concern to system designers and operators. During the social unrest of the 1960's, concern arose over the physical security of computer systems. They were expensive and visible symbols and, consequently, attractive targets for sabotage. Later, concerns over privacy and an awareness of increasing incidents of financial computer crime motivated the managers to take a more sophisticated look at protecting their systems and data.

Classifications of Computer Security

Security experts distinguish between three types of security: *physical, procedural,* and *technical.*

Physical security refers to techniques that physically isolate a computer system from access by unauthorized persons. It also includes protection of the facility from external dangers such as earthquake, fire, flood, or power failure.

Procedural security is the set of rules by which a system operator manages the system personnel and the flow of work in the organization. It can include such measures as preemployment screening of staff, work assignments that minimize opportunities to act in inappropriate ways, auditing procedures, and controls on the flow of work through the system.

Technical security refers to the software and hardware controls set up within the system itself. Techniques used to provide security may include cryptographic encoding of data, complicated access and identification procedures, and hardware which is dedicated to the auditing function.

Some security experts claim that too much attention on technological fixes has distracted system operators from more traditional but effective measures they could be instituting. However, the increased proliferation of small systems and the trend toward communication-based systems are making technical security more important. The techniques of physical and procedural security are well-understood and translate relatively easily from the noncomputer world into that of the system operator. Technical security, a newer area of research, is less understood, but is related directly to the problems of system design.

Computer scientists have proved that it is theoretically impossible to achieve perfect security inside the program itself. That is, it cannot be demonstrated that any particular combination of hardware and programing is proof against some new unexpected type of attack. Improving the security of a computer system involves balancing the costs of protection against the expectation of loss resulting from the threats and vulnerabilities. While it cannot provide a final answer, R&D in the field of computer security can substantially decrease protection costs.

Risk analysis, the process of weighing all these factors in a decision model, is a difficult job. The precise factors are unknown, and it is difficult to determine whether all possible alternatives have been covered. Research can develop techniques for performing risk analyses with greater precision, and the Government has new research and standards activities in this area. While the standards are directed at Federal systems, they will provide useful guidance to the private sector.

Technological instruments for security fall into three categories, according to the intent of the designer: *prevention, detection,* and *auditing. Prevention* means keeping unauthorized persons from having access to the system, and keeping authorized persons from using the system wrongly. *Detection* means catching an unauthorized procedure when it is attempted and preventing its completion. *Auditing* means the determination of whether unauthorized acts have occurred. A particular security technique is usually directed toward one of these goals.

Specific Techniques of Security

Authentication: The first objective of security is to assure that only authorized personnel can access the system. *Identification* is the process of establishing a claim of identity to the system, either with a name or an account number. *Authentication* is the process of verifying the claim.

The simplest and oldest procedure is to use a password or number that is known only to the individual authorized to use the system. The *personal identification numbers* assigned to bank customers for use on ATMs are examples of such codes.

The security provided by password schemes is limited, although more elaborate versions offering some improvements have been developed. However, the security of any password scheme depends fundamentally on the ability and willingness of the user to keep the code secret.

Physical identification techniques, which depend on measuring certain personal physical characteristics, are being developed for use as authenticators in computer system access. To be useful, any such system must be able to discriminate between persons, but at the same time be insensitive to changes in the characteristics of a particular individual over time.

The system operator, when selecting an authenticating technology, has to make a choice in balancing two types of errors—classifying a fraudulent identity as correct (type I) and classifying a proper user as fraudulent (type II). These two types of errors have costs associated with them, and are usually at opposite ends of a tradeoff curve for any specific technology. The type I error can be minimized only at the cost of maximizing the type II error, and vice versa.

Fingerprints: The technology exists for reading and encoding fingerprints with minimum delay, but the devices are expensive (over $50,000). Although the pattern is complex, fingerprints can be encoded in a computer using less than 100 characters by storing only certain key data points. This storage efficiency means that a complete set of fingerprints for every person in the United States could be stored easily in a commercially available bulk memory.

The cost of directly reading fingerprints, however, seems to suggest that it will not become a widely used method of authentication, at least in the near future. Its use will be restricted to very high security requirements, and to applications where fingerprints themselves represent significant data, such as in police work.

Hand Geometry: A new and surprisingly effective form of physical identification is the geometry of the hand. Individual finger lengths vary from one person to another. This variance is sufficiently significant and unique to be the basis for a relatively inexpensive (around $3,000) identification device. It is based on the use of a high intensity light shining on a pattern of photocells. It is sensitive both to external geometry and to the translucence of the flesh near the fingertips. Thus, it is quite difficult to deceive it with any artificial device.

Voice Recognition: Research on the techniques for voice analysis and voice synthesis has resulted in methods for distinguishing individuals by their speech. In these systems, a random list of words is shown to the individual, who then speaks them into a microphone. By having the computer generate a new list each time, the system makes it impossible for an imposter to use a tape recorder to fool the system.

The system has high interpersonal discrimination, but seems to be weaker on intrapersonal differences. It may reject authorized persons suffering from colds, hoarseness, or even emotional tension.

Voice recognition systems are not yet commercially available, although at least one firm, Texas Instruments, has installed a home-developed system for use in their facilities.

Since information collection is relatively cheap, requiring only a standard microphone, amplification, and signal conversion hardware, the limitations of the technology seem to be in the computational techniques. As software improves, and as the cost of computer hardware drops, voice recognition could become a popular low-cost authentication technique.

Signature Verification: Passive signature verification uses pattern-recognition techniques to analyze and encode a signature on a check or form. It is a difficult task, because a signature can vary depending on an individual's mental and physical state, the type of writing implement used, and because forgers can be quite skillful. One company has announced a product for providing passive signature verification for bulk application, particularly the processing of checks. It is not clear whether such technology is operationally effective in identifying forgeries, and whether it could be reduced in cost sufficiently to be used at the point of sale.

Dynamic signature verification systems track the actual path of the pen point as the individual creates a signature. Sensitive instruments measure variables such as the pen's speed and acceleration, the amount of time the point remains on the paper, and the changing pressure on the point. Several organizations, including IBM, are working on dynamic identification; however, no products are as yet commercially available. Some experts judge this to be a promising technology.

Much R&D is aimed at finding a more reliable substitute for the currently used magnetic cards and passwords to identify and authenticate individuals. To date only a few products have come on the market, and those have been designed for use in applications with very high security requirements. The cost limitation seems to depend on the characteristics of the sensor, since the microprocessor costs have dropped so low. No doubt a growing demand could motivate a flurry of new products in the early 1980's.

The amount of data required to store computer representation of the pattern for any of these candidate technologies is relatively small—a few hundred characters. Thus any of them, if they become widely implemented, could become the basis for a quasi-universal identification code used by all private and Government organizations.

Encryption

In the past, cryptography was principally a tool for military and diplomatic communication. Now, however, modern data communication systems increasingly are transmitting private information of high value, and the need to protect these communications from interception and manipulation has prompted an explosion of interest in civilian encryption.

A standard for encryption technology, the Data Encryption Standard (DES), has been established by the National Bureau of Standards for Federal use. It is apparently also being widely adopted in the private sector, since several commercial manufacturers are producing devices based on it. While some experts have questioned the robustness of DES, it seems to have been accepted generally as an inexpensive technology that is at least effective for low- or middle-level security needs.

Another set of techniques that has received some attention lately has been labeled "public key" encryption. The idea behind these codes arose from basic research in computational complexity, a field of computer science dealing with possible theoretical limits on the ability of even the most powerful computers to compute certain mathematical solutions. A public key code uses one key to encrypt and another to decrypt a message. Knowledge of the encryption key is no help in deriving the decryption key, even though their mathematical relationship is known. Thus, the security of the code does not depend on the security of either the encoding key or of the secrecy of the mathematical relationships. Since one of the major problems in the use of cryptography is control of the key itself, a system in which the decoding key need not be known even to the data sender is promising for many applications.

Public key codes also promise to be useful in electronic message systems, since they can be used for authenticating messages in the absence of signatures. Several applications of this sort have been proposed. However, public key codes are in their infancy, and it is not known with certainty whether unanticipated problems will arise as they are used.

Encryption has uses other than merely securing communications. Used internally in a computer system, it can isolate sets of data from unauthorized users. It can also allow users to enter data but not to read it, or to read but not modify data. It can even separate the activities of various connected computer processors.

Authorization

Most large-scale information systems are designed to serve several users simultaneously. The data bases in the machine often contain clusters of information that serve multiple needs. It is necessary, then, to control the access of users who are authorized to be on the machine, but may not be authorized to have access to specific parts of the data.

For each user, the system must keep track of which parts of the file can be accessed and manipulated, and what forms of access are held (read the data, enter new data, and so on). The system also must control the giving of permissions. Can one user, who is authorized to see a file, give access permission to another user? There are many situations in which this is a legitimate and even necessary procedure, yet it complicates enormously the problems of access control. Researchers are developing ways to model these assignments mathematically and avoid unexpected loopholes in system access control.

The continued growth in the size of information systems and in the numbers of people allowed to access them will continue to put pressure on system designers by complicating the authorization process.

Logging

Logging is the process of auditing the accesses made to a data base by all users. Systems for keeping a complete or partial record of all access to the data have received more attention since privacy has become an issue. The system operator needs to account for all accesses made to files of personal data. Since the log itself is a file that contains potentially sensitive personal information, the need to protect it may be even greater than that for the original data base. For this reason, some experts suggest the use of a separate small machine to monitor accesses to the data base.

The system operator can then examine the log for unusual patterns of file access or other significant actions of the users that may indicate that unauthorized use is being made of the system. When it is possible to code certain unusual patterns of use, the logging system itself can be programed to watch for those events. It will then either send a warning to the system operator, or call on a special security surveillance program that collects as much detailed information as possible about the transaction.

Operating Systems

The operating system of a computer, the set of programs that control its work, is the fundamental piece of software on which all other application programs depend. Consequently, the integrity of the operating system is a necessary prerequisite for any other software security. Although no system can be designed to be perfectly secure, there is much that can be done to construct highly secure systems.

R&D is ongoing in this area, and results will be slowly incorporated into existing systems. However, progress will be hindered by the difficulty in adapting current operating system programs. These contain millions of instructions, and have been modified and expanded over several years by many programers. The systems are difficult to change, as are the habits of their users.

Some computer installations still use operating systems written nearly 20 years ago. Computer operators fear that disruption and trauma would result from adopting radically different operating systems, and manufacturers resist compromising investments amounting to billions of dollars that they have made in existing programs. Thus, the most acceptable new techniques over the short term will be those that can be adapted to existing systems. However, it is the very size, complexity, and growth history of these current systems that create their greatest weaknesses—the logical holes and flaws through which a determined outsider can gain access.

Data Base Security

As data bases grow larger and are designed to serve multiple purposes, the likelihood increases that system operators will want to grant selective access. The problem is difficult. In an employee data base, for example, it may be desired to allow the personnel department access to some records, the finance department to others, and the medical department to still others.

One of the major problems is that of authorization determining which user can do what. Another related issue is how to structure the data base to allow such authorizations to be enforced. The question of which controls are even possible is, in itself, a complicated one. Research in data structures is developing new techniques which will probably come into use rapidly as new data base systems come on the market.

Encryption is one technique that will be used increasingly in cases where different groups of data and their users can be easily partitioned in terms of access control. It will be less useful when the data are highly integrated, and when it is not known during the design stage where boundaries will eventually be drawn.

Years ago, some hope was placed in the use of so-called "aggregated files," particularly when used for research with sensitive personal data. These files supposedly eliminate problems associated with maintaining personally identifiable data by stripping off identifiers and lumping them together in statistical clusters. It has been shown, however, that aggregating data statistically does not always assure that a clever inquirer cannot reverse the process and derive substantial personal information. In the same way, merely stripping identifiers off records of personal information may not preserve the integrity of the information, for a surprisingly small amount of descriptive information can serve to identify an individual uniquely. R&D is being conducted on ways to transform data bases collected for social research purposes so that the individual information is completely obscured, but statistically relevant calculations can still be done.

Chapter 14
Industry Structure

Contents

LIST OF TABLES

Chapter 14
Industry Structure

Introduction

In less than 30 years the electronic data processing (EDP) industry has grown to be a major economic sector of the economy. The total revenues for the industry worldwide were estimated to have been over $60 billion in 1979. The U.S. industry share of this market was about $46 billion.

The top 20 domestic companies in the EDP business in order of size are listed in table 9. Some of these firms are also engaged in other types of business, but only their EDP revenues are shown. The total EDP revenues in 1979 of the leader, IBM, were over $18 billion, nearly eight times those of the next largest company, Burroughs. Revenues of the eighth company, Hewlett-Packard, were nearly twice those of the ninth, Memorex.

The top eight companies are those marketing full lines of general purpose computers, referred to in both the industry and this report as *mainframe computers.* The rest succeed, in general, by focusing on a more limited market sector—very small machines, very large machines, specialized peripheral hardware, or various types of computer services.

The companies examined in this study range widely in size. While the market is clearly dominated in terms of size by the top eight (70 percent of the total revenues), much of the significant market shifting and innovation that will affect the future of computer use are taking place among the smaller companies. It has been estimated that there are over 4,000 firms in the EDP industry.

Growth in the hardware side of the industry will continue but not spectacularly. Rapidly decreasing prices for hardware will be more than offset by increased sales. How-

Table 9.—Top 20 EDP Companies in 1979

Rank	Company	1979 EDP revenues ($ million)	Percentage: Domestic market	Percentage: Principal product
1	IBM	$18,338	46%	Mainframe computers
2	Burroughs	2,434	59	Mainframe computers
3	NCR	2,404	46	Mainframe computers
4	Control Data	2,273	68	Mainframe computers
5	Sperry Rand	2,270	55	Mainframe computers
6	Digital Equipment	2,032	62	Mainframe computers
7	Honeywell	1,453	67	Mainframe computers
8	Hewlett-Packard	1,030	52	Minicomputers
9	Memorex	664	51	Memories
10	Data General	540	73	Minicomputers
11	Storage Technology	480	88	Memories
12	Xerox	475	85	Peripherals
13	TRW	440	77	Services
14	Texas Instruments	425	82	Minicomputers, terminals, and consumer goods
15	Computer Sciences	415	88	Services
16	Automatic Data Processing	401	92	Services
17	GE	350	79	Services
18	Electronic Data Systems	312	96	Services
19	3M	310	81	Peripherals
20	Northern Telecom	300	65	Peripherals

SOURCE: *Datamation,* July 1980, pp. 98-99.

ever, those companies using new computer and communication technologies to provide innovative information services to individuals and business will grow the most rapidly.

The advent of the microcomputer and low-cost digital communication opens new opportunities to entrepreneurs. Microprocessors lower the cost of system implementation to a mass-marketable level; and readily available, inexpensive communication technology provides a mechanism for mass distribution that has been lacking in the past.

These developments do not necessarily imply that the principal participants will change drastically over the next 10 years. The large EDP and communication corporations have been highly adaptable, and can be expected to move into these new services. The traditional information firms, researchers, and publishers are merging with the newer, high technology computer and communication companies. For example, ABC has bought MacMillan Press. On the other hand, Dun & Bradstreet, an established retailer of information, has purchased National CSS, Inc., a major supplier of computer programing and time-sharing services, and Readers Digest has purchased The Source, a new on-line information service.

This emergence in the 1980's of technology-based information service industries as a major business sector is significant both with respect to an overall analysis of market trends and for this assessment. The nature and social consequences of these new services are likely to have a major impact on Federal policies concerned with information and information processing. The form and availability of these services will, in turn, be affected by Government policy.

A final important characteristic of the U.S. computer and communication industry is its major role in the international market. International sales are concentrated among the top nine corporations, which average from 40 to 50 percent of all the foreign sales. The smaller firms are much less active internationally, probably because they view the domestic market as adequately rewarding and because of the high cost and uncertainty surrounding the marketing of high technology abroad.

Computer Hardware

The computer industry has been highly segregated along product lines for some time. Several companies manufactured so-called "super computers." Along with a few other firms, they produced a full line of small to large systems. Others specialized in minicomputers. However, the lines between these major categories have blurred as many intermediate size systems, both general and special purpose, have arisen to fill the gaps. The needs of computer users have also shifted substantially, creating more opportunities for small specialized companies to develop.

This evolutionary shifting of products, producers, and user needs makes difficult any attempt to chart historical trends for a particular class of machine. For example, the minicomputer of today is, in some ways, more powerful than a large computer of several years ago. Companies such as Texas Instruments, that used to sell only electronic components for computers, now market entire systems.

The principal characteristics of the computer hardware industry are summarized in table 10 (also see tables 11, 12, and 13). For analytical purposes, the industry has been divided into six sectors. Although the boundaries between them are vague, these sectors are generally recognized by the industry.

The principal characteristics of change in the computer hardware industry are the following:

Table 10.—Computer Industry Structure

Characteristics of hardware	Purpose and/or use	Nature of present industry	Nature and size of present market	Future trends
Microcomputer The smallest sized computers; can fit on one circuit board, and soon on a single silicon chip; inexpensive.	Used as "intelligent" components for games, appliances, watches, etc., or as the heart of larger general computing systems.	Modest to small companies in terms of electronic data processing revenues.	Growing rapidly; over $1 billion by the early 1980's. United States leads with increasing competition from West Germany and Japan.	Growth rate between 30 to 40 percent per year. Sales growth from $100 million in 1977 to $1 billion in early 1980's. Small firms being acquired by large international conglomerates.
Personal or desktop computer (see table 11) Small, but fully capable computer systems, costing several hundred to a few thousand dollars.	For use by individuals in the home, in business, or in school.	Many small entrepreneurs—"a cottage industry." Very successful entry by a consumer electronics retailer, Tandy (Radio Shack).	Individual users. Storefront and mail order sales. 1979 sales of $500 million.	Explosive growth of market in next few years. Possible acquisition by large consumer product firms and retailers emulating Tandy success.
Minicomputer (see table 12) Small computer systems selling for less than $50,000.	Designed to be used for a dedicated set of applications with informal, hands-on access.	Mix of large and small companies. Has provided opportunities for new entrepreneurs such as Prime Computer.	Shipments of $4.3 billion in 1979. Worldwide market growth rate for past several years of 35 percent.	Growth rate will slow to 25 percent per year; relative flattening of market in 1980's; software gaining in importance. Fewer new entrants.
Mainframe computer (see table 13) Medium- to large-scale computer systems, costing from a few hundred thousand dollars to several millions.	General purpose computers, usually serving several users and applications.	Dominated by several large corporations, with IBM the revenue leader by a wide margin.	The bulk of general computer sales—$8 billion in 1979.	Continued steady growth, with no major changes in relative positions of the top seven companies. Increased foreign competition.
Plug compatible computer Electronically equivalent to the equipment of other manufacturers—usually IBM.	Same as above, but with potentially better performance, better delivery, or lower price than IBM offers.	A very few companies concentrating narrowly on particular market opportunities.	Appears to be surviving new IBM product announcements and growing. Strongest growth is in specialized systems.	Risky market, very sensitive to IBM product and price announcements. Not likely to become a significantly large industry, but to prod big companies through competition.
Supercomputer Extremely large, powerful computers.	Predominantly for scientific and technological applications requiring large amounts of computing and data analysis, e.g., meteorological forecasting.	A few companies—most specialize in this type of system.	Small, specialized market, estimated at about $500 million.	Market growing more diversified. Will continue to be important but relatively small. IBM may bring in a totally new system; potential growth of foreign sales.

SOURCE: Office of Technology Assessment.

Table 11.—Desktop and Personal Computer 1980 Worldwide Shipments

By units	***444,000 units total***
Tandy-Radio Shack	25%
Commodore	23
Apple	17
Hewlett-Packard	6
IBM	2
Others	27
By revenue	***$1.9 billion***
Hewlett-Packard	21%
Apple	10
IBM	9
Tandy-Radio Shack	7
Tektronix	3
Others	50

SOURCE: International Data Corp., *1981 Computer Industry Briefing Session,* p. D-8.

Table 12.—Minicomputer and Small Business Computer 1980 Worldwide Shipments

Minicomputer[a]	
By units	*137,000 units*
Digital Equipment Corp.	44%
Data General	14
Hewlett-Packard	8
IBM	7
Honeywell Information Systems	4
Others	23
By revenue	*$6.35 billion*
Digital Equipment Corp.	34%
Hewlett-Packard	16
Data General	11
Honeywell Information Systems	7
IBM	6
Others	26
Small business computer[b]	
By units	*71,000 units*
IBM	33%
Others	23
Digital Equipment Corp.	12
National Cash Register	11
Wang	8
Burroughs	7
Data General	6
By revenue	*$3 billion*
Others	33%
IBM	28
National Cash Register	10
Wang	10
Digital Equipment Corp.	8
Burroughs	7
Data General	4

[a]International Data Corp., *1981 Computer Industry Briefing Session,* p. D-4.
[b]International Data Corp., *1981 Computer Industry Briefing Session,* p. D-6.

Table 13.—Computer Mainframe 1980 Worldwide Shipments[a]

Rank	Company	Revenues ($ millions)	Percent
1	IBM	$10,650	62.4%
2	HIS	1,550	9.1
3	Sperry Univac	1,410	8.3
4	Burroughs	1,000	5.9
5	NCR	480	2.8
6	CDC	400	2.3
7	Amdahl	380	2.2
8	DEC	205	1.2
9	National	190	1.1
10	Cray	50	0.3
11	Magnuson	35	0.2
12	IPL	10	0.1
(b)	Compatible peripherals	700	4.1
	Totals	$17,060	100.0%

[a]Shipments of large general purpose computers only. Companies listed may derive significant additional revenue from shipments of other types of computer systems.

[b]Value of shipments of plug-compatible peripherals produced by many smaller companies.

SOURCE: International Data Corporation, *1981 Computer Industry Briefing Session,* p. C-3.

- The mainframe business is still the major component of computer sales and will be for the foreseeable future. IBM has the largest market share by far, and there is no evidence that its lead is shrinking.
- The growth rate for sales of very small systems—desk-top or personal computers—will be very high, while the historically high rates of growth for larger systems will level off somewhat.
- In response to the changing nature of the computer marketplace, more emphasis will be placed on retail marketing and customer services. Retail firms not traditionally associated with computers will enter the small computer field.
- The explosive growth of the microprocessor industry may be slowed by limited production capacity and by the increasingly high costs of design and tooling for new applications.
- There has been recent evidence of a trend toward acquisitions of small semiconductor companies by large firms. According to one report, of 36 new semi-

conductor companies formed since 1966, only seven remain independent. Many of the acquisitions have been by foreign firms: French, West German, Japanese, Canadian, and Dutch.

- While foreign competition has made some inroads in electronics sales, and computer manufacturers are wary, particularly of Japanese competition, no evidence of any substantial impact on the domestic computer hardware market exists at present. The microprocessor and personal computer markets seem to be most vulnerable to such threats.
- Particularly in the small machine and special application markets, there appears to be wide opportunity for entrepreneurs to innovate and make a successful market entry.

Auxiliary Equipment

Many companies have successfully competed in the computer market by providing the peripheral equipment—terminals, memories, and the like—that extend the capabilities of existing computer systems. This independent peripheral market can be roughly divided into two parts—equipment in direct competition with that offered by the system vendor, and specialized hardware not commonly manufactured by the mainframe companies.

Most mainframe computer companies sell a wide range of peripheral devices for information storage and for input and output of data. However, other manufacturers claim that by specializing in some specific category of device they can offer better quality at a lower price. Often, in fact, these units are sold to the computer system manufacturer, which in turn puts its own name on them. The total auxiliary equipment market is estimated at around $7 billion or more. Thus, even though the major mainframe manufacturers take a large portion of that market, the remainder is well worth competing for.

The categories of equipment shown in table 14 below are not a complete list. The range of accessory equipment sold for computers is extremely wide.

The industry for auxiliary equipment has the following principal characteristics:

- All of the major manufacturers offer a wide assortment of peripheral equipment for use with their systems, and the sale of this equipment constitutes a major portion of the market. However, there is an active and profitable group of independent manufacturers selling equipment of all types. In many cases, the large computer corporations have an agreement whereby they purchase this independent hardware and put their own brand name on it.
- Users are more likely to accept new and improved devices as they come on the market, because it is much easier to change auxiliary equipment with minimum disruption of their operations. Furthermore, different auxiliary equipment can perform an identical function with a greater variety of possible internal technologies and designs. These two advantages lead to market opportunities for inventors and, hence, to profitable new enterprises.
- Much of the interest in the area of data storage is concentrated on large and inexpensive bulk memories. Current activity is in bubble memory and floppy disk technology, although the use of the video disk for very cheap data storage is also being explored and appears likely in a few years.
- The terminal industry is growing quickly, matching the growth in the use of

Table 14.—Auxiliary Equipment Industry Structure

Characteristics of hardware	Purpose and/or use	Nature and size of present industry	Nature and size of present market	Future trends
Random access memory devices				
High-speed, usually uses large-scale integration technology (500+ circuits on a single chip); recently IBM introduced very large-scale integration (VLSI) technology (several thousand circuits on a single chip). Connects directly to the computer processor.	The main storage for data while being used by the computer.	All computer manufacturers sell these as an integral part of their systems; also sold by some independents, mostly as IBM compatible equipment.	Market for independent vendors has developed, especially for IBM- compatible products.	Independents are motivated to develop products faster to compete with IBM's cheap VLSI technology. The market is risky due to the uncertainty over IBM's plans.
Bulk memory devices (a) Magnetic tape and fixed head disks				
Communicates with the central processor through an intermediary controller; has slower access times and larger capacity.	An auxiliary memory device to hold data not currently being used by the system.	Several independent manufacturers; very competitive. Major suppliers include firms such as Memorex, Storage Technology, 3M, Xerox, and Ampex.	Independents can serve a larger potential customer base than any mainframe vendor, because they can design high-performance equipment that can be interfaced with a variety of computer makes. Over $1.5 billion in sales.	Some improvements are still likely, but major breakthroughs are unlikely. It will still be a common technology during the next decade, but will eventually be replaced by electronic technologies.
(b) Floppy disks				
Inexpensive, easy-to-handle, and reliable form of bulk memory storage.	Originally developed by IBM as a control memory for the System 370 series of computers. At present, it is the medium-of-choice for small computer systems, intelligent terminals, word processing systems, and similar applications.	Successful area for small entrepreneurs. Leading independent producer is a small, California-based company, founded in 1973—with $18 million in sales that year. Presently, more than a dozen large and small manufacturers in the field.	Because of applications to small computers (see *Purpose and/or use* column), its market is somewhat different from the markets for the predominantly medium- and large-scale systems for magnitude tape and fixed-head disks.	The technology is developing rapidly, driven by competitive pressures, and the demand is growing due to the proliferation of small computers.
(c) Very large memories				
Stores trillions of bits of information. A few very different technologies are used, e.g., video tape and laser photographics.	Acts as an archive for very large quantities of data, where the information is rarely changed and infrequently accessed.	Very few manufacturers, principally Ampex and IBM.	Limited, special purpose market.	The demand for this type of storage will grow, but rapid growth will depend on the development of new technologies, such as holographic storage, and appropriate software techniques.
Graphical display equipment: (a) Video graphics				
Picture displayed on a cathode ray tube with the capability to display color and fully shaded solids.	Presents computer output graphically for such applications as computer-aided design. Users can interact with the display to control computation or put information into the system.	Has been domain of a few, small companies selling relatively expensive systems to a narrow range of users. As cost of electronics has dropped and more efficient graphics software has been developed, cost of graphics systems has decreased markedly.	The market for full video graphics is growing rapidly as graphics-oriented applications are becoming more accepted by users.	The further lowering of prices due to the economy-of-scale effect, along with the accumulation of experience are expected to increase market demand. Inexpensive systems are increasingly being incorporated into remote data terminals. The prediction is that by 1983, the market for all graphics display terminals will reach $500 million annually, and for graphical display equipment will grow to a billion dollars or more from the present quarter of a billion.

Table 14.—Auxiliary Equipment Industry Structure (continued)

Characteristics of hardware	Purpose and/or use	Nature and size of present industry	Nature and size of present market	Future trends
(b) Plotter graphics Picture is drawn by a mechanically controlled pen.	Gets graphical information out of a computer in the form of hard copy.	Dominated by California Computer Products (Calcomp). The plotters sold by most major computer vendors are made by this company. (Vendors put their own names on.)	The revenues of Calcomp exceed $100 million.	
Printers An alphanumeric text is printed on paper. Offers a wide range of speeds and technologies from impact printing to photo Xerox imaging.	The principal means of producing printed reports from a computer on paper.	Mainframe manufacturers dominate, but there are some successful entries by independents. The principal independent manufacturers are Centronics and Dataproducts.	The revenues of the principal independent manufacturers are about $100 million each.	The market is expected to reach $3.6 billion by 1985. The development of a reliable printer in the 1980's that would sell below $1,000 would tap rapidly expanding small computer markets, and would not compete directly with industry giants.
Data entry systems Includes these products: Keypunches (cards). Keyboard to tape and disk. Terminals—video and typewriter. Optical readers—bar code, marks, or characters. Magnetic character readers. Direct data recorders. Voice data entry.	Gets information into computers; optical and magnetic readers as well as direct data recorders transmit data directly to the computer from the source. For readers, the source is a machine-readable code, e.g., magnetic characters on a bank check and printed bar codes on grocery items. For recorders, direct measurements are made of physical properties, e.g., temperature and pressure. Voice recognizers convert oral communication to computer code.	Numerous small companies; IBM's domination through the emphasis on punched cards is fading as new, better technologies are coming into use.	Sales, which were about $1.77 billion in 1977, are growing at about 15 percent per year. The market for voice recognizers has been surprisingly good.	The market is expected to grow rapidly in the 1980's as the technology improves. Data recorders will become more important as computers are used for controlling processes both in industry and in the home.

SOURCE: Office of Technology Assessment.

communication-based computer applications. The current trend is toward graphical display, and putting more computer processing logic in the terminal itself.

- Data entry has been moving gradually away from the use of punched cards and toward the use of other media such as magnetic disks. The most significant trend in the 1980's will be toward systems designed to capture information directly from the source by voice recognition, by image analysis, and by direct measurement.

The Data Communication Industry

The data communication industry produces goods and services necessary to transmit digital data between computers or between computers and a terminal. For convenience, the industry is split into two sectors, the hardware manufacturers and the carriers, as shown in table 15. (The description of the industry presented in this study presents an information processing view. The OTA report on *Telecommunication Technology and Public Policy,* in press, presents a common carrier view of the data communication industry.)

The magazine *Datamation* estimates the total data communication industry to be running currently at over $4 billion per year, and to be growing rapidly. The carriers have most of the action, nearly three-quarters of the market; AT&T has the biggest individual share, about 56 percent of the total market. The top 10 companies (other than AT&T) in the data communication hardware market are listed in table 16, and the top 10 data carriers in table 17. All revenue estimates are from *Datamation.*

The following comments about the data communication industry appear pertinent:

- The most apparent characteristic of the data communication hardware market is the continued presence of IBM at the top of the list. Even though only one product covered in the survey is offered, a communication front-end processor, IBM's revenues are more than double those of the next largest company. Yet this income represents less than 1 percent of IBM's total corporate income.
- There appear to be many healthy small firms in the communication hardware business. Generally, they specialize very narrowly along specific product lines. Six of the 10 companies listed in table 16 are small firms earning most or all of their income in the data communication field.
- The entire market for data communication is still not very large compared with that for other services, principally voice. It is estimated at between $2 billion and $3 billion. Accurate numbers are hard to get, because the carriers themselves do not always know when their lines are being used to carry voice or data.
- Most experts expect a major explosion of the market for data communication over the next two decades. The most interesting developments are the plans of some very large corporations for providing sophisticated data communication services in the near future. Although behind schedule, AT&T's ACS (Advanced Communications System), should begin operation soon. IBM and Aetna are underwriting a new corporation, SBS (Satellite Business Systems), to provide such services. Exxon is reputed also to be planning services of this kind. A highly flexible system will be offered by these companies that is designed specifically for high-speed data transfer in many forms—e.g., com-

Table 15.—Data Communication Industry Structure

Characteristics of hardware	Purpose and/or use	Nature of present industry	Nature and size of present market	Future trends
Hardware manufacturers (table 16): (a) Front-end processors				
Small, specialized processors dedicated to controlling communications. They are located between the main computer and the communication network.	Control communications by handling all the messages between the main computer and the terminals.	IBM dominates with the 370X processor for its own machines. Other major computer vendors are also principal suppliers. The two largest independents are Comten, Inc., with over $37 million in front-end processor revenues, and Computer Communications, Inc., with over $17 million. The number of minicomputers bought to serve in this capacity cannot be estimated.	Total sales approached $400 million in 1979. Due to the growth of communication-based applications, an independent industry is arising to market these processors, which for many years mainframe manufacturers have been providing as standard add-on equipment for their machines.	Will grow rapidly, paralleling the trend toward the application of integrating data communication and computer systems.
(b) Modems and multiplexors				
Modems change the electric characteristics of the data signal to be transmitted on the communication line from digital to audio—to match the requirement of a communication system to transmit voice. Multiplexors mix multiple data messages into a single stream of information down the wire.	Adapt computer systems and terminals to the communication systems designed to carry voice.	AT&T is a major supplier of modems (estimates are that Bell has as many in use as the entire independent market). Multiplexors are supplied mainly by independent manufacturers, principally: Motorola, Racal-Milgo, General Data Comm, Paradyne, and Rixon. All but the first one are small companies with their principal revenues from this market.	1979 independent market estimated at over $450 million.	Similar to above, except that these functions may be included to some extent in new data communication services.
(c) Network/node controllers				
These are a recent concept, which look and perform very much like front-end processors. They are located within the communication network.	Principally control data flow through a complex network of computers and communication lines.	Supplier picture is not clear. It appears to be dominated by two independents, Comten and Computer Communications, Inc.	A new market, motivated by the evolution of distributed processing systems containing several computers interconnected on a communication network. In 1979 sales were about $70 million.	Similar to above.

Table 15.—Data Communication Industry Structure (continued)

Characteristics of hardware	Purpose and/or use	Nature of present industry	Nature and size of present market	Future trends
(d) Terminals Any human-operated input-output device through which information can enter or leave a communication network.	Connect a human user with a computer.	Appears to range from large, mainframe manufacturers to small specialist companies. Some merging may be possible between small computer and terminal industries, as terminals become more "intelligent" and small computers gain more communications capability.	Estimated to be large—over $1 billion—and growing rapidly. A vast market exists for high-quality, low-cost hard-copy printed output, now too costly relative to the small computer to which it may be attached. A high demand is anticipated for terminals, concomitant with a projected explosive market growth for small and networked systems.	Terminal costs will fall, but not as fast as electronics. "Intelligent terminals" will dominate the 1980's market, and be indistinguishable from small computers with communication capabilities. There will be a shift to more sophisticated graphics terminals. Capabilities, including color and half-tone, will be built into terminals, thus obviating the need for putting them on the main computers.
(e) Other devices A miscellaneous group of relatively cheap specialized devices, for managing and testing communication network.	These are for setting up and maintaining a data communication network. Includes such devices as those for monitoring communication lines for data accuracy and performance and those for tracing errors in a network system, also voice response units that interface a computer on one end of a telephone line with a human on the other.	Racal-Milgo and Northern Telecom, which largely produce test equipment, are the principal suppliers.	A still quite small market relative to the entire communication market, but amounts to over $100 million.	This will continue to be a relatively small market.
Data carriers (see table 17) The medium that is used to transport or carry communication data or information, e.g., AT&T long lines, satellites.	To transfer data such as computer data, electronic mail, facsimile, and video conferencing with a high degree of flexibility at high speeds.	Currently, AT&T is the principal data carrier. Most other major carriers (see table 17) also predominantly supply telephone service. A competitive industry of pure data communications is developing. The high capital requirement will keep the competition to a few large firms.	A large data communication market, ($4 billion in 1979) but still relatively small when compared with voice. Accurate figures are difficult to obtain since carriers often cannot distinguish whether their lines are carrying data or voice.	A major explosion of the data communication market is predicted over the next two decades. Some very large corporations are moving toward providing sophisticated data communication services in the near future. New services will be based on communication networks with substantial built-in "intelligence" allowing data storage for future retrieval.

SOURCE: Office of Technology Assessment.

Table 16.—The Ranking and Revenues of the Top 10 Manufacturers of Data Communication Hardware

Rank	Company	1979 revenues ($ million)
1	IBM	$158
2	Racal-Milgo	121
3	NCR	82
4	Motorola	81
5	Memorex	54
6	3M	49
7	General Datacom	42
8	Paradyne	41
9	Control Data	40
10	Rixon	36

SOURCE: *Datamation,* June 1980, pp. 120-121.

Table 17.—The 10 Leading Carriers of Digital Data and Their Data Communication Revenues

Rank	Company	1979 revenues ($ million)
1	AT&T	$2,309
2	GTE	798
3	Western Union	451
4	ITT World Communications	170
5	United Telecommunications	68
6	TRT	28
7	Tymnet	24
8	Continental Telephone	21
9	Central Telephone	20
10	WUI	16

SOURCE: *Datamation,* August 1980, p. 107.

puter data, electronic mail, facsimile, or video teleconferencing.

- These services will be based on communication networks that will have substantial "intelligence" built into them; thus, the services will not easily be classified as pure data carriage or as information processing. Since one industry (communication) is regulated and the other (data processing) is not, a complicated regulatory problem is created, the resolution of which will allocate a multibillion dollar market among competing industrial giants.
- The computer industry has two strong but contradictory reactions to these developments. They see the evolution of these new services as providing exciting possibilities for new computer-communication applications, some linked on a worldwide scale. Many of the new applications being planned will serve large multinational corporations or consortiums of smaller users, such as stockbrokerage houses.

On the other hand, some fear that a big winner of this competition for the data communication market would be a monopoly controlling all data communication services worldwide. While the carrier business is not a game for small players, such massive domination by one supplier could be threatening to the hardware and service sectors that are currently promising for the creative small business entrepreneur.

Special Applications

The emergence of microprocessor technology has led to a new type of industry that incorporates the processor into a device that performs a specialized function. This type of industry will grow rapidly during this decade, fueled by growing consumer demand for computerized products. Eventually, such markets for computers may dominate the industry and become analogous to those for electric motors. Few consumers purchase them directly, but buy many products in which they are incorporated.

Some of these products will be full computer systems programed to perform specific jobs; for example, the word processing applications discussed later. Others, such as the popular computer games, incorporate intelligence but do not look like computers. These applications are also distinguished from the incorporation of microprocessors in common consumer goods such as microwave ovens and automobile engines. The applications discussed here are new products, offering new, intelligence-based capabilities to their users. It is impossible to describe such an industry generically; therefore a few current examples are provided (see table 18) that illustrate the variety of ways in which this set of industries will develop. Clearly, the opportunities are endless for inventive novel applications of this new technology. The analogy mentioned above with the electric motor is particularly useful in picturing the future potential of this industry sector.

Array Processors: An array processor is a special purpose computational unit designed to solve specific types of mathematical problems. (See ch. 5.) It is normally attached to a general purpose computer system or minicomputer that sets up the data, feeds the problem to the array processor, and puts the answer out in appropriate form. Array processors have become particularly popular for research and engineering applications that involve signal processing or the modeling of large physical systems.

Over 15 firms market these units, ranging from IBM to small companies for which such a processor is the only product. The processors cost between $5,000 for a small unit on a printed circuit card to several million dollars for Control Data's Star computer. Many small companies (such as Floating Point Systems) and larger ones (such as Raytheon and Westinghouse), which don't engage in the general purpose computer business, have found the lower end (up to $150,000) of the array processor market to be attractive, and have thus far successfully competed in it.

Speak and Spell®: This is a specific product invention of Texas Instruments, which is a leading manufacturer of microelectronics. Unlike some of the other semiconductor companies, which sell their devices wholesale to other manufacturers for incorporation into products, Texas Instruments also produces a line of consumer devices that use their own electronics. These are largely centered on electronic hand and desk calculators and a recently announced personal computer.

In 1978, Texas Instruments produced a small hand-held device that combined their microcomputer technology with some new speech synthesis capabilities to produce a combination toy and teaching aid called "Speak and Spell®." The device speaks a word and the learner types the word into the machine on a small keyboard. "Speak and Spell®" was an instant success, encouraging Texas Instruments to plan not only improved versions of the original but to find other specialized products that combine speech synthesis and microcomputers.

Translators: The hand-held language translator is a new consumer device that has been appearing in the stores over the last 2 years. It resembles a pocket calculator but has an alphabetic keyboard and a somewhat longer display window. A person types in a word or phrase in one language and reads the translated phrase on the display.

The machine was invented by a small group of entrepreneurs who were not in the electronics business at the time. Forming a company called "Friends Amis," they developed the design and specifications of the logic chip required. They then contracted with a microprocessor manufacturer to produce the specialized electronics, and arranged with a distributor of consumer electronics to retail them under the distributor's brand name.

The translators were an instant hit, enough so that Texas Instruments and Lexicon have been drawn into the market. Despite the competition, Friends Amis has been a success, turning an initial investment of $1 million into an $8 million profit last year on sales of $30 million. Still growing, the company soon plans to market a hand-held computer through an agreement with Matsushita. The Japanese corporation will provide the marketing capability the small company lacks. Besides making money, Friends Amis has, in the words of Fortune magazine, "managed to father a new branch of consumer electronics."

Table 18.—Special Applications Industry (examples)

Characteristics of hardware	Purpose and/or use	Nature of present industry	Nature and size of present market	Future trends
Array processors Specialized units for very economic and fast solutions for particular mathematical problems. Usually attached to a mini- or general-purpose computer for control and input/output.	Research and engineering applications involving signal processing or modeling large physical systems.	Units marketed by over 15 firms from IBM to small companies with processor as their sole product. Cost from $5,000 for smallest unit on printed circuit card to several million dollars for the largest size. Opportunities for small entrepreneurs.	Research and engineering design laboratories are principal users.	More specialized designs targeted at unique types of calculations. The potential large revenues from such specialization will stimulate growth.
Speak and Spell® Consumer electronics device—small, hand-held, combining the manufacturer's (Texas Instruments) microcomputer technology with speech synthesis capabilities.	Combination toy and spelling teaching aid—machine speaks word, then child types it on small keyboard.	Specific product invention of Texas Instruments.	Instant consumer success.	The manufacturer will improve present product and develop additional specialized products combining speech synthesis and microcomputers.
Language translators Consumer electronics device—a hand-held language translator with an alphabetic keyboard and a display window similar to but larger than that on normal calculators.	Type in word or phrase— read off translation on display.	Developed by entrepreneurs originally not in electronics business who contracted electronics to microprocessor firms.	Consumer electronics success— company that developed product had $30 million in sales in 1979 on an initial investment of $1 million.	Consumer electronics market still growing—several electronics companies are entering. The unit may evolve into a more general, hand-held personal computer.
Word processors A computerized "intelligent" typewriter that stores a document electronically as it is entered, and displays the image on a cathode ray screen.	Allows operator to edit and correct text directly in memory, and automates repagination, hyphenating, and justification. Some systems can correct spelling.	Principally companies that make or have made computers, e.g., Wang, IBM, and Digital Equipment Corp. Other firms are now entering, illustrating new opportunities being opened by cheap electronics, e.g., Lanier Business Products, a leader in dictaphone sales. Also major firms such as Xerox and Exxon are developing strong positions.	Over 80 percent growth in 1979, growth expected to continue over 50 percent in 1980.	In 1980's integrated office systems will display sophisticated capabilities for correcting grammar and formatting text. They will merge with new data communication services linking geographically separated offices through high speed data communication networks offering video, audio, and computer conferencing, and distributed information processing. Electronic archival storage for storing and retrieving information efficiently and easily will be offered.

SOURCE: Office of Technology Assessment.

Word Processing Systems: These are important new applications around which a major industry will grow in the 1980's. Word processing systems, the first entry in the office automation trend, are designed to increase the productivity of information handling by automating its preparation and flow. The applicable technologies will be drawn from both computers and communication, and the trend will be toward the integration of document preparation, storage, and transmission.

For now, the principal offering on the computer side is the word processor. It is essentially a computerized, intelligent typewriter that stores a document electronically as it is entered, displays the image on a cathode ray screen, and allows the operator to edit and correct the text directly in its memory. Tedious tasks such as repagination, hyphenating, and justification are taken care of automatically. Some systems even correct spelling, and some observers expect systems in the 1980's to display sophisticated intelligence for correcting grammar and formatting complicated text. The market for sophisticated word processing systems grew over 80 percent last year, and next year market growth should still be over 50 percent.

The principal actors in the word processing business have tended to be companies that make or have made computers, such as Wang, IBM, and Digital Equipment Corp. However, other firms are now entering the market, illustrating the opportunities for new entries being opened by cheap electronics. Lanier Business Products, for example, a leader in the sale of dictaphones, has entered with both stand-alone systems and those using a shared computer that serves several terminals. Lanier, principally viewed as a firm with marketing expertise, purchased interest in a small data products company, AES Data Ltd., that designs and manufactures the word processing equipment.

The most important trend that experts think will dominate in the 1980's is the merging of these word processing systems with the new data communication services being planned, such as SBS or AT&T's ACS. Using these new services, geographically distributed organizations will be linked together through a very high speed data communication network offering video and audio conferencing, computer conferencing, and distributed information processing.

The final ingredient for the integrated office systems of the next decade is the development of electronic archival storage. The hardware base exists for storing information at a cost lower than that of filing paper. The need now is for appropriate software that would allow the user to store and retrieve information efficiently and easily. Some systems are on the drawing broad. Systems Development Corp. and Datapoint have announced prototypes for systems they will sell in a year or so.

As these trends merge, whether small firms can continue to successfully develop and compete in the word processing market may depend on the degree to which interfaces become standardized, allowing competition for particular components of an integrated office system. Major firms such as Xerox, IBM, and Exxon have taken aim at the automated office market, and competition will be severe.

Computer Services

The computer services industry, summarized in table 19, performs a wide variety of tasks that make the computer more accessible, more usable, and/or less expensive for computer users. Some companies sell time on their own computers; others provide programing or operations services (including training, consulting, and facilities manage-

Table 19.—The Computer Services Industry Structure

Services provided	Purpose and/or use	Nature of industry	Nature and size of market	Future trends
Processing services These firms, called service bureaus, provide access to computer time. They also provide access to programs designed for specific control applications.	For computer users preferring to purchase computer time from outside firms rather than owning and operating their own systems.	A relatively few very large companies and a large number of small but profitable operations. (See table 21.) Good opportunity for small companies to compete successfully by taking advantage of specialized services targeted at a market in which they have particular expertise.	About $6.7 billion worth of computer time was purchased in 1980, and the market is growing at nearly 20 percent per year.	The coming generation of cheap computers will be a threat to those companies that just provide computer time without adding market value in the form of application packages and consulting. Consequently, the move is toward providing programing and other support activities that are less sensitive to the specific source of computer power.
Professional software products and services: Prewritten programs to do specific tasks that can be leased or purchased by users. Because heavier program development costs can be written off against multiple users, this commercial software can be more soundly based mathematically, more flexible, more reliable, and better documented than a home-grown program would be. In addition, the vendor assumes the burden of the continued maintenance and improvement of the package.	***(a) Software products*** The majority are for applications, although some are designed to improve the operation of the user's system. They tend to be large and complex, designed for broad applicability, e.g., large data management and file inquiry systems, optimization programs, and packages of sophisticated statistical routines.	A large number of small firms. Over 90 percent of the companies fit into ADAPSO's category of those that are smallest in size. The large hardware vendors also sell some software products tailored for their machines.	For the total software products industry, the market is estimated at over $1.5 billion per year.	The growth rate for the next 5 years for this unusually fast growing industry is estimated at 30 percent.
(b) Software services Provides programing expertise to develop a specific program for a particular user.	For a user's own projects, and to assume the responsibility for the major development efforts for which the customer does not have the appropriate staff.	A few small companies specialize in programing. Many large firms, hardware manufacturers, service bureaus etc., offer programing services to support their customer's needs.	A market about equal to that for prewritten packages. It is estimated at around $1 billion per year.	The industry predicts substantial growth of over 20 percent annually for the next few years, depending in part on the continued scarcity of skilled talent, which makes it costly, thus discouraging users from establishing their own staff of application programers. More market segmentation and specialization seems likely.
Other services The industry provides a variety of support services to users.	For consulting, for operating the customer's computer center, for maintaining the hardware, and for integrated hardware/software systems.	Mostly very small firms.	No solid estimates of market size could be comparable to that of professional software support market.	A new service industry is developing providing books, magazines, software, exchange services, employee education, and consulting, for small computer users. With the increase in the use of small computers in the 1980's, some major growth potential may exist for services designed to make these new systems most useful to a new class of inexperienced users.

SOURCE: Office of Technology Assessment and Association of Data Processing Service Organizations.

ment) to users who own their systems. Still others sell prewritten programs or provide access to those programs on a service bureau computer. Most recently, some companies offer processing services through integrated hardware/software systems.

The Association of Data Processing Service Organizations (ADAPSO) is the principal organization representing this industry. They define the role of their industry as adding "value to the computer hardware utility by integrating into the service people, expertise, products, distribution networks, and education." The structure of the computer service industry as discussed here reflects, in part, that used by ADAPSO.

The largest publicly held independent computer service corporations along with their estimated 1979 revenues from computer services are shown in table 20.

Table 20.—Estimated 1979 Revenues for the Top Five Independent Computer Service Companies[a]

Company	Estimated 1979 revenues ($ million)
Automatic Data Processing	$372
Computer Sciences Corp.	343
Electronic Data Systems	274
Tymeshare	193
Bradford National	120

[a]The three companies with the largest computer services revenues—IBM, Control Data Corp., and Burroughs—derive their primary revenues from hardware sales and thus are excluded from this list.

SOURCE: Association of Data Processing Service Organizations.

Table 21 shows the structure of the computer services industry in terms of size of firm.

The following observations can be made about the computer services industry:

- The availability of inexpensive capable computer hardware will put pressure on service firms that only provide customers with access to computer time. Even so, most observers do not expect the computer service bureaus to fold up.
- The service bureaus are showing a trend toward offering an integrated set of services based not only on access to pure computing services, but also to specialized programs and data bases already present in the company's system.
- The service industry seems to be characterized by a few large firms and many, equally profitable, very small operations serving very specialized markets (such as law firms, pharmacies, and civil engineering firms). The development of new data communication facilities will make more of this type of specialized service possible by providing a national marketplace for it.
- A new industry will develop to support the personal and desk-top systems now being marketed. These services will offer maintenance, programs, consulting, and education specifically oriented to owners of these very small systems.

Table 21.—Industry and Revenue Structure of Computer Services Industry[a]

Size of operation	Number of companies	1979 revenues ($ billion)	1979 gross profit margin (percent)	Growth rate (percent)
Over $25 million	40	$ 4.0	10%	20%
Between $10 million and $25 million	70	1.5	7	23
Between $2 million and $10 million	450	2.0	9	22
Under $2 million	3,500	2.5	9	22
Total	4,060	$10.0		

[a]This table includes estimated revenues for computer services provided by independent computer service companies and computer hardware manufacturers. Numbers are rounded off.

SOURCE: Association of Data Processing Service Organizations.

Information Services

Selling information is a centuries-old business; however, the computer is forcing a radical change in the character of this industry. The nature of the information sold, the way it is provided, and the principal organizations supplying information services are all changing rapidly, which will shape a new type of industry in this decade.

The traditional information industry has always been predicated on the assumption that some information has tangible economic value and can be treated as a commodity. The industry, taking this traditional approach, views itself as similar to any other industry in structure. That is, it is divided into producers, distributors, and retailers. For example, an author might be a producer, a publisher, a distributor, and the bookstore the retailer. Similarly, in broadcasting there are show producers, networks and syndicates that distribute the programs, and the local stations that broadcast them into homes.

Now the industry is computerizing. Traditional information organizations such as Dun & Bradstreet, Macmillan Press, and the Knight-Ridder newspaper publishers are exploring new uses of information technology to expand their offerings. On the other hand, computer service bureaus, as pointed out in the previous section, are moving away from offering pure computer time and toward providing program and data services that are certainly classifiable as information services even by the most traditional standards. Finally, new companies such as Data Resources, Inc. (now part of McGraw-Hill) have been formed specifically to provide computer-based information services. The computer's impact is being felt by all three sectors of the information industry.

In the *production* of information, increased computerization of social activities means that there is a swiftly growing pool of information of all kinds that can be read by a computer. Financial information, airline reservations, stock transfers and commodity prices, and even wire service news, are examples of information already available in electronic form. Much of it is already transmitted on communication lines.

The next decade or two will see most of the information needed to run people's lives and businesses originated and stored in computers. This trend will stimulate the distribution and retailing of information, because putting the information into computer readable form is a major cost of current automated information services.

Data communication technology is changing the rules for the *distribution* of information. Traditional distributors such as broadcast networks, book publishers, and common carriers are looking carefully at the potential advantages offered by data communication. The publishers see a new mechanism to distribute newspapers, books, and magazines, in addition to possible new services; the common carriers and broadcasters see new uses for their facilities as vehicles for these services.

Many of these services will soon be retailed directly to the home or office via telephone, television, and cable. Precursors to these services already exist in a few local cable systems, and experiments such as the recently canceled AT&T Electronic Information Service provide an automated telephone directory and a selection of other information systems over a telephone line to a home terminal.

Some information services are transformed by the use of technology, others are created. It is the new computer-based services that are of particular interest to this study.

The Information Industry Association identifies nine categories of information industry. These are:

1. producers of primary information (books, journals, research studies, etc.);

2. producers of secondary information (indexes, bibliographies, data bases, microforms, directories, etc.);
3. communication companies (broadcast, cable, switching, etc.);
4. information distributors, agents, or brokers (on-line service, sales representatives, dealers, etc.);
5. information transactors (banks, lending institutions, investment houses, etc.);
6. consultants or contract suppliers of information (designers, developers, etc.);
7. information retailers or outlets (on-demand services, search services, etc.);
8. equipment or supplies companies (computers, micrographics, text processing, graphic arts, etc.); and
9. popular media organizations (news, education, advertising, etc.)

Some of these classifications are of particular interest to the computer and communication industry.

Producers of Primary Information: For some time, the intermediate processes of publishing have been undergoing automation. Computerized typesetting, on-line editing and other uses of word processing, and digital communication of edited text are being widely adopted and should increase productivity substantially.

For the time being, the final product will continue to be in paper form. However, the future widespread use of the video disks and high-speed data communication systems may gradually lead to products being published in digitized formats as well.

Producers of Secondary Information: Many producers of bibliographies and information directories now regularly prepare them on computers. Some even offer the final product on-line from a computer. The user dials in from a remote terminal to get the desired information.

These industries have found the computer to be useful not only to automate the more routine aspects of their operations, but also to provide more sophisticated analyses and customized arrangements of the information they maintain. Since a large on-line data base can be searched far more effectively by computer than by hand, the services provided by such a producer are qualitatively different from those provided by a traditional bibliographic service.

Such information, however, is currently very expensive to prepare. Persons must first read the printed material, then analyze, index and otherwise code it, and put it into machine-readable form. In the future, when most printed text will originate on computer-based text processors, automated computerized indexing systems will eliminate most of these tasks.

This high labor cost, coupled with the fact that the initial significant market for such systems is the research community, means that most bibliographic systems now available were originally supported, at least partially, by the Federal Government. Some are now self-supporting, while others continue to be subsidized, depending on their purposes. Bibliographic information is the hardest case, however.

There have been some successful entrepreneurial experiments in providing other forms of on-line data service. Data Resources, Inc. (DRI) is one of the best known. Founded by the well-known econometrician, Otto Eckstein, DRI provides econometric data and access to sophisticated computer-based models to economists, particularly those in private industry. Most of the major corporations in the United States now subscribe to DRI's services.

There are a number of such firms that have been founded to provide computerized databank services. Many are still quite small, specializing in particular types of data to serve narrowly targeted markets. The range of services is quite broad. One industry analyst identified 22 different categories of databank service.

Data Transactors: There are many firms that create useful information in the course of their business, although they may not be in the primary information business. For example, banks, stockbrokers, airlines, and credit card companies all create transactional information. More and more of this information is in computer-readable form and, furthermore, is possibly valuable to some other party. This firm or individual may be in a related business, or may have no connection with the principal field of the original data collector.

The market for such data is likely to grow significantly over the next decade. Pools of data from transactions will accumulate in computer systems, and new enterprises will spring up to collect, organize, and sell them. The transactors will find that wholesaling their data pools to such firms will be a profitable side business. When that happens, pressures may well build to increase the amount of information collected beyond that necessary to serve the immediate transaction, thereby increasing the resale value of a company's data pool. These firms will then become principal actors in the information industry.

Information Retailers: Information retailers provide computer-based information products directly to the business or private consumer. They may also be the producers, or they may simply retail other producers' products. So-called "videotext" service providers, which offer in-home information over broadcast or cable television channels, usually serve as brokers, making their facility available to anyone who wants to provide an information service, in the same way that a grocery store carries soup made by different producers.

Many of the databank providers discussed in the section on secondary producers offer very complicated systems that require some training and experience to use. Therefore, these services are often provided through an intermediary, such as a consultant, librarian, or stockbroker. In a sense, these persons serve as retailers of the information service, marketing it to individual users. The characteristics of the information services sector are summarized in table 22.

The following conclusions can be made about the information services sector:

- Traditional information producers such as book publishers, newspapers and network broadcasters will be converting their services into computer and telecommunication-based offerings.
- New information services will be transmitted to the home over telephone, cable, and broadcast carriers. Some of these services may be integrated with in-house computer systems and video disk and tape units.
- Libraries will extend their services beyond mere provision of books into offering computer-based services. Such new activities may conflict with the new commercial in-house services mentioned above.

Table 22.—The Information Services Industry Structure

Nature of the information	How information is provided	Nature of industry and/or market	Future trends
Producers of primary information			
Published materials.	For time being in paper form.	Traditional book, magazine, and newspaper publishers.	The increasing adoption of computerized typesetting, on-line editing and other uses of word processing, and digital communication of edited text should substantially increase productivity. The future widespread use of video disks and high-speed data communication systems may gradually lead to the publication of products in other digitized formats such as in-home video information systems.
Producers of secondary information			
Bibliographies, information directories, econometric data, and other particular types of data that serve narrowly targeted markets—over 22 different categories of data bank services have been identified. Most are prepared on a computer.	On paper and on-line from a computer. The user dials in from a remote terminal to get the desired information.	Most bibliographic systems available were originally supported, at least in part, by the Federal Government, because their initial chief market was the research community. Some are now self-supporting; others, depending on their purpose, continue to be subsidized. Data Resources, Inc., is an example of a successful entrepreneurial experiment in providing other forms of on-line data services—econometric data and access to sophisticated computer-based models for economists. Many small firms have been founded to provide a broad range of computerized data bank services.	Most of this data will reside in computer systems to be called up as needed by customers.
Data transactors			
Firms create useful transactional information in the course of carrying out their business, e.g., banks, stockbrokers, airlines, and credit card companies.	Most is in a computer-readable form that may be of value to some other firms or individuals.	Currently, the number of transactors is growing but there is only a small market for their data.	Pools of data from transactions will accumulate in computer systems, and new enterprises will spring up to collect, organize, and sell them. Transactors who profit from wholesaling their data pools to such firms, will be motivated to increase the quantity of information collected in order to raise the resale value of their data pools. These firms will then become principal members of the information industry.
Information retailers			
Computer-based information products.	Directly to businesses or private consumers.	Retailers may also be information producers or may just retail the products of other producers, e.g., so-called "videotext" services that offer in-home information over broadcast or cable television channels, usually serve as brokers who make their facilities available to anyone wanting to provide an information service.	Computers are having the effect of blurring the distinction between the products and services offered by the computer industry. This new hybrid industry will offer new forms of information services, marketed in new ways, to new users.

SOURCE: Office of Technology Assessment.